The Place-Names of the Isle of Wight

OTHER BOOKS ON PLACE-NAMES FROM 'PAUL WATKINS'

Richard Coates, *The Ancient and Modern Names of the Channel Islands. A Linguistic History*

Sylvia Laverton, *Exploring the Past Through Place-Names: Woolverstone*

Joyce Miles, *A Dictionary of House Names* (forthcoming)

W. F. H. Nicolaisen, *Collected Essays on Scottish Place-Names* (provisional title, forthcoming)

Adrian Room, *The Street Names of England*

Alex Rumble and A. D. Mills (eds), *Names, Places and People: an Onomastic Miscellany in Memory of John McNeal Dodgson* (forthcoming)

Jeffrey Spittal and John Field, *A Reader's Guide to the Place-Names of the United Kingdom. A Bibliography of Publications (1920-1989) on the Place-Names of Great Britain and Northern Ireland, the Isle of Man and the Channel Islands.* An updated *Supplement* to this is forthcoming

Finally, 'Paul Watkins' is also the distributor of *Nomina*, the journal of the Society for Names Studies of Britain and Ireland. Volumes 1 to 16 are all available and we have recently produced a catalogue of the journal's contents. A catalogue of our medieval history titles is also available.

THE PLACE-NAMES OF THE ISLE OF WIGHT
Their Origins and Meanings

A. D. Mills

PAUL WATKINS
STAMFORD
1996

© 1996 A. D. Mills

Published by
PAUL WATKINS
18, Adelaide Street
STAMFORD
Lincolnshire, PE9 2EN

ISBN

1 900289 00 8

Typeset by the publisher
from the disc of the author
in Times New Roman

Printed on permanent paper

Printed and bound by Woolnoughs of Irthlingborough

CONTENTS

Acknowledgements 6

Introduction
    Scope and arrangement of the book 7
    Wight place-names and their meanings 8
    The chronology and language of the names 10
    Some different place-name types 13
    Wight place-names and the landscape 15
    Wight place-names and history 16
    Wight place-names and people 18

Alphabetical list of Wight place-names 21

Glossary of the elements found in Wight place-names 115

ACKNOWLEDGEMENTS

This book could not have been brought to its present form without the valuable assistance and advice of Mr C. D. Webster, County Archivist at the Isle of Wight Record Office in Newport. He has most generously provided me with many new spellings and identifications, as well as corrections to Kökeritz and information concerning manorial and family history. My warmest thanks are due to him for giving me the benefit of his expertise and of his vast knowledge of the local records. However I do of course take sole responsibility for the views finally proposed in the book, as well as for any errors or deficiencies remaining.

I would also like to thank my good friend Mr Clifford Arndt-Snelling for his expert advice and considerable help with the word-processing of the book.

The book is dedicated to my dearest wife Solvejg
in gratitude for her patience, love and loyal support

INTRODUCTION

Scope and arrangement of the book
The place-names of the Isle of Wight are an important, colourful and distinctive part of its rich heritage. They are as full of fascinating variety as its scenery and landscape, and even the most familiar names will often have an unexpected origin and meaning. This book sets out to provide all those who know Wight, whether fortunate enough to live here or only passing through as visitors, with information about the origin of its place-names, their history, their underlying meaning, and their significance in the Island's story.

The alphabetical list of Wight place-names includes all the names mentioned on the latest edition of the 1:50000 map published by the Ordnance Survey in the Landranger Series (No. 196), with the addition of many names from other maps. Thus besides all names of towns, villages and hamlets, the list includes names of rivers and streams, hills, woods and archaeological sites, as well as many names of farms, mills, bridges, bays, promontories and other features of the Island landscape.

Each entry in the list provides the basic information about the history and origin of the name, as far as it is known:
(a) its modern form as it appears on map or signpost, with some indication as to its location with reference to some nearby place;
(b) a selection of representative early spellings (printed in italics) for the name, with dates, to show how the name has developed (when the name occurs in a particularly interesting early record, like a Saxon charter or Domesday Book, this is mentioned);
(c) the probable original meaning of the name, deduced from those early spellings and presented as a 'translation' into a modern English phrase of the old words or 'elements' that make up the name;

THE PLACE-NAMES OF THE ISLE OF WIGHT

(d) the elements or personal names from which the name is derived, cited in their original spelling and language (the elements are also listed in the Glossary at the end of the book);
(e) other brief comments where appropriate on points of linguistic, geographical, or historical interest.

Each name has been freshly interpreted in the light of all the evidence so far available – documentary, linguistic, topographical, historical and manorial. The pioneering and detailed treatise by the Swedish scholar Helge Kökeritz, *The Place-Names of the Isle of Wight*, published as long ago as 1940, is still often valuable for its philological insights. However the present book has naturally benefited from the vast amount of research done on English place-names over the last half century, as well as from a great many recent publications on the Island's history. It has been possible to consult important documents not used by Kökeritz such as the Tithe Award maps and apportionments in the Public Record Office. Moreover the resources of the County Record Office at Newport, together with the enormous local knowledge and expertise of its archivist, Mr C. D. Webster, have been kindly placed at my disposal. Thus it has been possible to antedate many of Kökeritz's earliest spellings, often by several hundred years, to revise and correct some of his identifications, and in the light of these and other factors (such as manorial and family history) to suggest revisions or refinements of many of his etymologies. In particular, based on the very feasible suggestions of Mr C. D. Webster, it has been possible to put forward three important new identifications for Domesday Book manors (see the entries for Apse, Hill Farm in Brading, and Hulverstone).

Wight place-names and their meanings
Most people will have wondered at some time or other about the original meaning of a place-name. Why Cowes, Carisbrooke or Clamerkin? What is the origin of a name like Ryde or Mottistone? How did Bembridge, Blackgang or Totland get their names? What does Chale or Shanklin mean?

In fact all of these Wight names, like most of the names listed in this book, have original meanings that are not at all apparent from their modern forms. That is because most place-names today are what could be termed 'linguistic fossils'. Although they originated as living units of speech – coined by our distant ancestors as descriptions of places in terms of their topography, appearance, situation, use,

INTRODUCTION

ownership or other association – most have become, in the course of time, mere labels, no longer possessing a clear linguistic meaning. This is perhaps not surprising when one considers that many place-names are a thousand years old or more, and are expressed in vocabulary that may have evolved differently from the equivalent words in the ordinary language, or that may now be completely extinct or obscure. It is only by tracing each name back to its earliest spellings in the records that its original meaning can be discovered and its original significance appreciated.

Of course some place-names, even very old ones, have apparently changed very little through the many centuries of their existence, and may still convey something of their original meaning when the words from which they are composed have survived in the ordinary language (even though the features to which they refer may have changed or disappeared). Thus old Wight names like Brook, Freshwater, Newchurch, Northwood and Sandford are shown by their early spellings to be virtually self-explanatory, having undergone only minor changes in form and spelling over a long period.

But even a casual glance at the alphabetical list of Wight place-names will show that such instant etymologies are often a delusion. The modern form of a name can never be assumed to convey its original meaning without early spellings to confirm it. We find, for instance, that Loverston is not named from its lovers, that Scotland does not take its name from the Scots, that Apesdown has no connection with apes nor Stagwell with stags, that there never was a haven at Havenstreet, and that Bathingbourne has nothing to do with bathing in the stream! Instead these place-names, like many others, derive from old words or personal names which have come to resemble other words as the place-names have evolved over hundreds of years.

Names then can never be taken at their face value, but can only be correctly interpreted after the careful scrutiny of the earliest attested spellings in the light of the relevant linguistic, historical and geographical factors. This is best illustrated by comparing pairs of apparently identical names that prove to have quite distinct etymologies. Thus Alverstone in Brading differs in origin from Alverstone in Whippingham, even though each is named after an early Saxon lord of the manor. Rew Down and nearby Rew Farm near Ventnor contain quite different Old English words. Likewise Cheverton in Shorwell and Cheverton near Shanklin have totally

THE PLACE-NAMES OF THE ISLE OF WIGHT

different meanings, the latter being a manorial name ultimately derived from the former.

The Isle of Wight has its share of names, some of them very old, that are to be found in other parts of England. Names like Binstead, Compton, Hamstead, Kingston, Knighton, Newport, Preston and Wootton occur in other English counties, and their origins are usually straightforward. However a good many Wight place-names are quite unusual, and indeed unique to the Island, often containing rare old words found in very few other English names and usually now obsolete. These include Brading, Hardingshute, Lessland, Mottistone, Ningwood, Pidford, Shanklin, Shide, Sibdown, Vittlefield, and many others. Here again, it is only through early spellings that probable etymologies can be arrived at. For some names, of course, even early spellings do not always provide a clear unambiguous etymology, hence the good number of names for which alternative, or only tentative, explanations are suggested. Particularly common are names like Ashey, Bagwich, Budbridge, Chilton, Hoxall, Nunwell and Ramsdown, where the first element could be either a significant word or a personal name.

The chronology and language of the names
Most of the Wight place-names so far mentioned are of Old English or Anglo-Saxon origin. This is the overwhelmingly dominant stratum in the older place-names of the Island, as of other southern English counties apart from Cornwall, and in the case of Wight is the legacy of two closely related Germanic peoples, the Jutes and the Saxons. The archaeological and historical evidence suggests that the Jutes colonized the Island during the 6th century, establishing an independent province with its own kings which was eventually conquered by the West Saxons in the year 686 during the reign of Cædwalla of Wessex. It was also during the late 7th century that the hitherto pagan Jutes were converted to Christianity.

The names of Old English origin vary in age, and it is not always easy to tell which names belong to the earlier and which to the later part of the period. Some of the oldest names in Wight may well date back to the early Jutish phase of its history (that is from the early 6th to the mid 7th century), although most probably originated during the later West Saxon phase (from the late 7th century onwards up to the Norman Conquest). What is certain, however, is that names recorded in Domesday Book (compiled in 1086) or earlier, apart from the even

INTRODUCTION

older Celtic names mentioned in the next paragraph but one, will have had their origins in the Old English period. Even names that are first recorded in a 12th or 13th century source will often have been coined in Old English times, since the date of earliest occurrence of a name in a surviving manuscript is largely a matter of chance.

An enormous number of Old English words survive in fossilized form in the place-names of Wight as of other English counties, as will be evident from the Glossary of elements at the end of the book. Some of the oldest like *brerd* 'hill-side' in Brading, *ceole* 'ravine' in Chale, *clater 'loose stones' in Clatterford, *corf 'gap' in Corve, *horte* 'whortleberry' in Hardingshute, *scīete 'nook' in Shate and Sheat, or *scīd* 'plank' in Shide, are relatively rare in other parts of England, and most probably belong to the ancient Jutish/Saxon dialect of Wight. Indeed many other such old words found in the place-names still actually survive in local dialect use, like *shute* 'steep hill' (in The Shute and Barrack Shute), *rithe* 'small stream' (in Ryde), *plash* 'small pool' (in Plaish).

However the oldest place-name included in this book is almost certainly Wight itself. This ancient name is of British or Celtic origin, and thus predates the coming of the Jutes, appearing indeed in records as early as the 2nd century AD. What is interesting is that such a Celtic name should have survived the Jutish and Saxon colonization, providing at least some evidence of continuity and contact between the Celtic-speaking British inhabitants and their English-speaking conquerors. There may be other traces of this ancient Celtic stratum of names in Carisbrooke and Calbourne, both of which may be hybrid compounds consisting of an old Celtic river-name to which an Old English element has been added. The name Solent is another ancient name, certainly pre-English though its origin and meaning remain uncertain. It should perhaps be noted that although the Island was annexed by the Roman general Vespasian in about 43 AD and there is much archaeological evidence for the Roman presence here over the next three centuries, this presence did not result in any place-names that have survived.

Only a few place-names in Wight, as in most other English counties, are French in origin, in spite of the far-reaching effects of the Norman Conquest on English social and political life and on the English language in general. It is clear that by 1066, most major settlements and landscape features already had established names, and the new French-speaking Norman aristocracy only rarely gave

THE PLACE-NAMES OF THE ISLE OF WIGHT

French names to parts of their estates. However, Quarr (the site of an Abbey founded in 1132) and Beaper are purely Norman-French names, as is Freemantle which may in fact have been transferred from a place in France. The old name for Newtown, *Francheville*, is also French in origin, and Whitecliff is *la Blaunche Faloyse* in a 14th century source. Moreover the Norman-French influence shows itself in other ways: French Mill indicates early occupation by a Frenchman, Preston and Weston were called *Preston Vavasour* and *Weston Braybeof* in medieval times from the Norman-French family-names of their manorial lords, and many names have 'Frenchified' spellings in early medieval sources, especially in Domesday Book in forms like *Lacherne* for Kern, *Alalei* for Lea or *Lamore* for Moor (even though these are names of solidly Old English origin).

Of course, not all the names on the modern map, even names of sizeable settlements or well-known features, are as old as most of those so far mentioned. Beside the French names already noted, many names for settlements, farmsteads and topographical features originated in the Middle English period, that is between the 12th and 15th centuries inclusive. Names probably coined in this period include Apesdown, Bembridge, Cowes, Dolcoppice, Fullholding, Grange, Havenstreet, The Needles, Newchurch, Pagham, Parkhurst, St Helens, St Lawrence, and Tyne Hall.

Finally there are some place-names which originate in the post-medieval period or even in quite recent times. Many names of farms and holdings, derived from the family-name of an early owner or tenant, date from around the 16th or 17th century. Examples include Bachelors, Bartlett's, Blakes, Cassys, Clamerkin, Dallimores, Deacons, Harts, Hebberdens, and Rowlands. Many names referring to fortresses, mansions or other buildings belong to this modern period (Fairy Hill, Newbarn, Sconce Point), as do some names of suburbs (Lowtherville, Pelhamfield, School Green), commemorative names (Keats Green, Nansen Hill, Prince's Green, Tennyson Down), and transferred names (America, Bohemia, Egypt, London, and St John's Park). Many coastal names like Foreland, Puckaster Cove, and Warden Point are first recorded in the 16th and 17th centuries, and others like Reeth Bay, Scratchell's Bay and Steel Bay not until much later, but it should be noted that some of these may be much older than their earliest recorded spellings suggest. Indeed the same goes

INTRODUCTION

for other names first recorded at a relatively late date, like Dunsbury, Sainham, and Upton.

Some different place-name types
Wight is notable for its many names of 'simplex' type, that is short names that consist of only one element, such as Apse, Brook, Chale, Kern, Lake, Lynn, Ryde and Shide. The reason for this is no doubt the relatively small and compact size of the Island, making further descriptive or qualifying words less necessary for identification.

Nevertheless by far the majority of Wight place-names are of the 'compound' type, that is they consist of two elements, the first usually qualifying the second. Typical examples are Calbourne, Freshwater, Mottistone and Yaverland. Of course many of these have undergone some degree of reduction or contraction since they were first coined. Names like Appleford, Arreton, Osborne, Rill and Staplers have been considerably reduced by centuries of use in speech, although others like Bathingbourne still retain a more conservative spelling in spite of a much reduced local pronunciation. A common characteristic of compound names is the shortening of original long vowels and diphthongs as in compound words in the ordinary vocabulary. Just as *holi-* and *bon-* in the compounds *holiday* and *bonfire* represent *holy* and *bone* with their historically long vowels, so in compound place-names Old English elements like *bēan* 'bean', *dūn* 'down', *gāt* 'goat', *hām* 'home', *prēost* 'priest' and *stān* 'stone' occur with shortened vowels in names like Binstead, Dunnose, Gatcombe, Hamstead, Preston and Standen.

This tendency for long vowels to be shortened in compound place-names, together with weakening of stress at the end of names, resulted in some originally distinct elements coinciding in form and pronunciation. Thus it is not possible to be sure whether a number of place-names, such as Billingham, Newnham and Sainham, contain the important (and often early) Old English habitative element *hām* 'homestead, village' or the quite separate topographical element *hamm* 'enclosure, river-meadow'. The same factors lead to the confusion of *-ton* from *tūn* 'farm', *-don* from *dūn* 'down' and *-den* from *denu* 'valley' in names like Chellerton, Chiverton, Standen and Warden, and there are similar reasons for the replacement of *-mere* by *-more* in Leechmore, *-ham* by *-down* in Sandown, *-worth* by *-wood* in Dungewood, and *-ore* by *-worth* in Elmsworth.

THE PLACE-NAMES OF THE ISLE OF WIGHT

A particularly early and interesting type of Old English place-name is that sometimes called the 'folk-name', in which the settlement is named from the group-name of the settlers themselves. Brading 'the dwellers on the hillside' is the only example of this type in Wight. However other place-names likely to belong to the early part of the Old English period are those consisting of the name of a tribe or family of settlers with another element, such as Atherfield, Bathingbourne, Farringford, Horringford, Whippingham and Wilmingham.

Some names which go back to the Old English period still contain archaic grammatical features of the pre-Conquest language. The medial -n- that survives in names like Bouldnor, Dodnor and Gurnard is what remains of an old genitive (i.e. possessive) ending of the so-called 'weak' noun or personal name in Old English, and in Newnham the medial -n- is a survival of the old dative singular ending of the 'weak' adjective. Other names containing parts of old grammatical endings include Noke and Tyne Hall. The old spoken dialects of Wight are also reflected in the form and development of some place-names. For instance, Niton seems to contain an old Jutish form of the word 'new'; Pan, Black Pan and Walpan all exhibit a distinctive form of the word 'pen'; Kennerley and Lessland contain a dialectal -e- for Old English -y-; and the development of initial V- in Vittlefield and of initial Y- in Yafford, Yarbridge, Yarmouth and Yaverland are also typical features of the old local dialect. Some Old English words found in Wight place-names which still survive in the local dialect, like *plash*, *rithe* and *shute*, have already been mentioned.

There are numerous instances among Wight place-names of the workings of a process sometimes known as 'folk etymology'. This is a tendency for a name to be rationalized or reinterpreted once its original meaning has been obscured or lost – because words have gone out of use, or because the person commemorated in the name has been forgotten, or because of changes in pronunciation or spelling. Two particularly good examples are Centurion's Copse and St Martin's Down. In the first a real saint has disappeared to be replaced by a bogus Roman, and in the second a bogus saint replaces an old word for 'butter'! Among the other instances of folk etymology are Apesdown, Bathingbourne, Dolcoppice, Golden Hill, Havenstreet, Nettlestone, Puckpool, Stagwell and Whale Chine. In all these names, familiar words which are quite unhistorical but which make a kind of

INTRODUCTION

sense, have replaced unfamiliar or obscure words, or words which have undergone phonetic change. Folk etymology sometimes results in a phenomenon known as 'back-formation' – in Wight this has produced the two river-names Yar, each formed independently of the other from two different place-names.

Wight place-names and the landscape
The place-names of Wight reflect every aspect of its varied scenery and landscape, seen through the eyes of its earlier inhabitants. The importance of rivers and streams for early settlement – providing fertile soils and a good water supply – is reflected in the number of Wight places named from the rivers and streams on which they are situated, among them Brook, Calbourne, Carisbrooke, Freshwater, Lake, Lynn, Nunwell, Osborne, Ryde and Shorwell. The numerous places that take their names from fords and bridges, like Budbridge, Clatterford, Farringford, Kitbridge and Yafford, show the early importance of river crossings for communications and trade. Creeks and estuaries give name to Shalfleet and Yarmouth, and many other names refer to springs, pools, weirs and other watery features.

Other topographical features – hills and downs, valleys and hollows, moors and marshes, bays and promontories – are well represented among the names, as will be appreciated by a glance through the Glossary of elements at the end of the book. It will be apparent that our early ancestors made use of a vast topographical vocabulary, each word probably carrying fine distinctions of meaning which may be partly lost to us now. And as might have been expected, its island character makes the coastal names of Wight a particularly abundant group, marked by their great variety and including many that have a colourful figurative quality (Cowes, Goose Rock, Horse Ledge, The Needles, Puckaster Cove, Scratchell's Bay, Shanklin, Sugar Loaf). Another large group is of names indicating woodland, or clearings in woodland (among them Appley, Borthwood, Lea, Lee, Ningwood, Parkhurst, Rookley and Wootton), these reflecting a period when wooded areas were much more extensive than they are today.

The natural history of the Island is also well represented among its place-names. At least a dozen different species of tree are evidenced (in names like Apse, Birchmore, Heasley, Noke, Thorley and Wellow), as are many names of plants (in Cockleton, Hardingshute, Headon and Nettlecombe). Animals occur in names

THE PLACE-NAMES OF THE ISLE OF WIGHT

like Haslett and Rancombe, birds in Cranmore, Culver Cliff, Kitbridge, Rookley and Wroxall, insect life is represented in Cheverton and Emmethill, and other creatures mentioned include frogs (Froglands), toads (Padmore) and leeches (Leechmore).

Wight place-names and history

Wight place-names provide a great deal of information about its social, economic and cultural history. They reflect the many and varied aspects of human activity on the Island during the different historical periods – settlement and landholding, the establishment of Christianity, the economic exploitation of land and sea, the development of defensive forts and beacons, communications and trade, agriculture and industry. Many names refer to particular kinds of habitation or settlement, such as those containing the common element *tūn* 'farmstead, manor, estate' (Adgestone, Cockleton and some forty others), as well as those from *hām* (Whippingham, Wilmingham), *hām-stede* (Hamstead), *port* (Newport), *strǣt* (Havenstreet), and *wīc* (Week, Bagwich). Various kinds of domestic building are represented by *bōthl* (Buddle), *court* (Downcourt, Bridgecourt), *place* (Pitt Place) and *hūs* (Woodhouse).

Many Island place-names have religious associations. Early church buildings are evidenced in the names Bonchurch and Newchurch, church dedications give name to St Helens and St Lawrence as well as to St Boniface Down, St Catherine's Down and St George's Down, and priests are referred to in Presford and Preston. Many other names recall the vast estates on the Island held by the great abbeys and monasteries in medieval times, among them Apesdown, Combley Grange, Compton Grange, Grange, Holyrood Street, Lower St Cross Farm and Monktonmead.

Names from *burh* and *burh-tūn* like Stenbury and Barton Manor are interesting since they suggest early fortified sites, and old names like Chessell (the site of a 6th century pagan Jutish cemetery), Gallibury, Harboro and Mottistone also have important archaeological implications. Other Wight place-names recall the existence of later forts and castles, among them the names of coastal promontories like Sconce Point, Old Castle Point and Round Tower Point which are all called after forts built in the 16th century as a defence against foreign invasion. Fort Albert, Fort Victoria and Golden Hill Fort refer to 19th century coastal forts, and Barrack Shute recalls the site of a barracks used during the Napoleonic Wars. Other place-names, like Beacon

INTRODUCTION

Alley, The Nodes and Nodewell, Nodes Point, Totland, Wackland and Weards Cottage, are a reminder of the extensive beacon system of defence, well developed by the early 14th century, set up to give warning of invasion and other emergencies.

Many names provide information about the agricultural economy of earlier times. Different words for man-made enclosures include *worth* (Dungewood), *hæg* (Ashey), *penn* (Walpan), *pund* (Pound Green), **lycce* (Lessland), *tēag* (Tyne Hall) and *croft* (Whitecroft). Various other kinds of land-use are indicated by names containing elements like *feld* (Atherfield), *hamm* (Sandown), *land* (Fleetlands), *mǣd* (Monktonmead), **winn* (Winford), *lēah* (Barnsley), *lǣs* (Gotten Leaze) and **niming* (Ningwood). Some names refer to the kind or quality of the soil (Blacklands, Redhill, Sandhills, Whitefield). Among the Island names referring to crops are Berryl and Bierley (barley), Binstead (beans), Holden (hay), Rill (rye), and Watchingwell (wheat), whilst other food products enter into names like Appleford (apples), Perreton (pears), Hunning Hall and Hunny Hill (honey), and St Martins Down (butter). Names like Gatcliff and Gatcombe (goats), Lambsleaze (lambs), Osborne and Sheepwash (sheep), and Yaverland (boars), are a reminder of the importance of livestock to the Island's economy.

Some names contain elements which suggest the importance of communications and trade in early times. These include elements like *port* (Newport), *key* (King's Quay), *hæfen* (Western Haven), *ford* (Briddlesford), *brycg* (Langbridge), *scīd* (Shide), and *weg* (Redway). Other names reflect local industries and occupations, like Quarr and Pitt Place (quarrying), Fishbourne and Werrar (fishing), Saltern (salt-making), Crocker Street (pot-making), Alum Bay (mineral extraction), Borthwood and Staplers (timber), and Kern, Mill Farm, French Mill and Yafford Mill (milling). The reed-beds that gave name to Landguard, Redway and Roud, and the river-barriers or hatches at Lukely Brook and Yafford must also have had a part to play in the local economy.

Wight place-names provide some fascinating glimpses into the social life of the Islanders, into their practices, customs and beliefs, at different periods of their history. Mottistone is so named from The Long Stone which marked an important judicial meeting-place in the Jutish/Saxon period. Golden Hill and Scotland refer to the payment of taxes or rents. Gallibury Hump and Gallows Hill are grim reminders of the violent punishments meted out to criminals in early times, and

THE PLACE-NAMES OF THE ISLE OF WIGHT

other names with gruesome connotations are Burnt House and Deadmans Brook. Puckaster Cove was thought to be haunted by a goblin, while Devil's Chimney, Devil's Punchbowl, and probably Scratchell's Bay, were associated with the devil. Smuggler's Path alludes to the smuggling once rife on the Island's south coast.

Colourful legends, perhaps like all legends with at least an element of truth in them, have attached themselves to some names, among them Frenchman's Hole, Lord Holmes's Cellar and Parlour, King's Quay, Monks Bay, Queen's Bower, and Stag Rock. A few names seem purely whimsical (Fairy Hill, Pigeon Coo, Pigtail), some complimentary (Fairlee), some decidedly derogatory (Cockleton, Fulford, Fullholding, Mount Misery). Others make allusion to pastimes as various as hunting (Parkhurst and Great Park, Rancombe, Rodge Brook), bull-baiting (Bull Ring), merry-making (Marvel, and possibly Vittlefield), and probably even love-making (Luccombe).

Wight place-names and people
Many persons and families from many different periods of history are in a sense recalled and commemorated in Wight place-names. Some of the men who bore Old English names, like the Beadda who gave name to Bathingbourne or the Wippa who gave name to Whippingham, may have been among the Jutish or Saxon leaders or chieftains who colonized the Island from the 6th century onwards. Most of these, however, like the Beorhtwīg of Brighstone or the Æfic of Adgestone, will probably have been thanes granted their estates by kings or bishops at a somewhat later date during the Old English period, that is between the late 7th century and the Norman Conquest. There are some thirty such place-names, incorporating the personal names of Jutish or Saxon thanes or landholders, on the Island. Of particular interest are the Brandr and Sveinn of Branstone and Swainston, for these are personal names of Old Scandinavian origin, almost certainly implying that these landholders were ultimately of Viking stock, perhaps granted their estates by the Anglo-Danish king Cnut or his sons in the early 11th century. Also to be noted are the two likely instances of women among these early landholders, the Ælfwynn of Alvington and the Ēadwynn of Eddington (for which see St Helens): they will not have been secular leaders, but rather the widows or daughters of thanes who had earlier been granted the estates in question.

INTRODUCTION

About most of the individuals from the relatively remote Old English period, nothing more is known other than what the place-names themselves tell us. But in later periods, from the 12th century onwards, Island families are likewise recalled in the place-names, and these families are often well documented in local records. Scores of such families, some very well-known, some fairly obscure, are represented in Wight place-names such as Cassys, Clamerkin, Dolcoppice, Havenstreet, Pallance and Warlands, each one indicating the ownership or tenancy of a holding or estate at a particular date. 'Double-barrelled' names with so-called manorial affixes, where the family name is added to an existing place-name, are rare in Wight. Indeed none actually survive as such, although Pagham was earlier *Merstone Pageham* (here the affix alone has survived), Preston was earlier *Preston Vavasour*, and Weston was once *Weston Braybeof.*

Some Wight place-names of more recent origin commemorate famous persons who have had association with the Island, among them royal personages (Queen's Bower, Prince's Green, Fort Albert and Fort Victoria), literary figures (Keats Green and Tennyson Down), and even a Norwegian explorer (Nansen Hill).

This Introduction has only touched upon a few of the points of interest arising from a study of the Island's place-names. Naturally much more information can be gleaned from the alphabetical entries themselves, as well as from the Glossary of elements at the end of the book.

ALPHABETICAL LIST OF WIGHT PLACE-NAMES

Adgestone (near Brading). *Avicestone* 1086 (Domesday Book), *Auicheston* 1198, *Avichestune* c.1220, *Auchestone* 1299, *Achestone* 1351, *Agestone* 1487. 'The farmstead or estate belonging to a man called Æfic', from Old English *tūn* and an Old English personal name.

Afton, Afton Manor, East Afton (near Freshwater). *Affetune* 1086 (Domesday Book), *Affetone* 1189-1204, *Afton* 1224, *Afetone* 1271, *Affton* 1279. 'The farmstead or estate belonging to a man called Æffa', from Old English *tūn* and an Old English personal name.

Albany Prison (near Parkhurst). Named from the former *Albany Barracks*, so called after the Duke of York and Albany. The new Albany Prison was begun in 1963.

Alexandrian Pillar or Hoy's Monument (near Chale). This 72-foot high monument on St Catherine's Down was put up by Michael Hoy to commemorate the visit to Britain of the Russian Czar, Alexander I, in 1814.

Alum Bay (near The Needles). First recorded on Avery's map of 1720, and appearing as *Allum Bay* on Andrews's map of 1769, so called from the large quantities of alum found here mined as early as the 16th century. Alum Chine in Bournemouth is also named from the mining of alum, used industrially in paper-making and leather tanning.

Alverstone (near Brading). *Alvrestone* 1086 (Domesday Book), *Alvredeston* 1289, *Alverdeston* 1336, *Alfredeston* 1346, *Alverston* 1535. 'The farmstead or estate belonging to a man called Ælfrēd', from Old English *tūn* and an Old English personal name.

THE PLACE-NAMES OF THE ISLE OF WIGHT

Alverstone Farm (near Whippingham). *Elwerdeston* c.1200, *Alwardestone* 1235, *Alwardeston* c.1247, *Ailwardestone* 13th century, *Alewerstone* 1429. 'The farmstead or estate belonging to a man called Æthelweard', from Old English *tūn* and an Old English personal name.

Alvington Manor Farm (near Carisbrooke). *Alwinestune* 1086 (Domesday Book), *Alwinton* 1227, *Alfington* 1279, *Aluintone* 1302, *Alvyngton* 1326. Probably 'the farmstead or estate belonging to a woman called Ælfwynn', from Old English *tūn* and an Old English personal name. The Domesday Book spelling points rather to a masculine personal name Ælfwine but may be an error for *Alwinetune*.

America Cottages & Woods (1 mile west of Shanklin). Recorded as *America* on Andrews's map of 1769. It has been claimed that the name may have been given when oaks from here were used for ship-building at the time of the American War of Independence, which began in 1775.

Amos Hill (in Totland). Recorded as *Ameshill* in 1608. A manorial name, indicating possession of lands here by a family called *Ame* or *Ames*.

Apesdown, Apes Down (2 miles west of Carisbrooke). *Abbessesdune* late 13th century, *montem Abbatisse* (Latin) 1299, *le Abbedessedon* 1335, *Apesdown* 1489. 'The down belonging to the Abbess', from Middle English *abbesse, abbodesse* and Old English *dūn*. Alice, Abbess of Wilton, was granted land in Carisbrooke in 1251. It will be noted that the spelling with *-p-* (for original *-b-*) does not occur until the 15th century.

Appleford, North & Upper, Great Appleford Farm (south-west of Godshill). *Apledeforde, Apleford* 1086 (Domesday Book), *Westapeldereforde* 1271, *Estapeldreford* 1275, *Appeltreford* 1290, *Appelderford* 1330, *Apleford* 1559. 'The ford where apple-trees grow', from Old English *apuldor* and *ford*. The division into the two manors of East and West Appleford was early, the latter probably being identical with the modern Upper Appleford.

THE DICTIONARY

Appley (in Ryde). *Appeley* 1219, *Great & Little Appley* 1769, *Appley* 1781. 'Wood or clearing where apple-trees grow', from Old English *æppel* and *lēah*.

Appuldurcombe House (ruin, near Wroxall). *Apldecumbe* 1189-1204, *Appeldercombe* 1270, *Apeldurecumbe* 13th century, *Appeltrecoumb* 1289, *Appuldurcombe* 1504. 'The valley where apple-trees grow', from Old English *apuldor* and *cumb*. This place is only 2 miles away from Appleford which contains the same first element, although in this name the full form of the word *apuldor* has been preserved. The ruined Palladian mansion here, a seat of the illustrious Worsley family, was built in 1710.

Apse Heath, Apse Manor Farm (west of Shanklin). *Abla* (sic) 1086 (Domesday Book), *Apse* 1100-7, *Hapsa* 1100 (in a 14th-century copy), *Hapse* 1235, *Apse* mid 13th century, *Apse (Heath)* 1769. '(The place at) the aspen-tree or white poplar', from Old English *æspe, æpse*. For the Domesday identification I am indebted to Mr C. D. Webster, who finds convincing evidence in manorial history for placing *Abla* (hitherto not satisfactorily identified) here. In fact it is not unusual for the Norman scribes of Domesday Book to confuse *s* for *l*, so that *Abla* is simply an error for *Absa* = *Apsa*. The manor house here dates from the early 17th century.

Arched Rock (near The Needles). Sometimes called *the Arch Rock*, an apt name for this huge offshore rock which once formed part of the cliff.

Arreton (medieval parish, south-east of Newport), **Arreton Manor**. *Eaderingtune* c.880 (in an 11th-century copy of King Alfred's will), *Adrintone* 1086 (Domesday Book), *Aretona* c.1145, *Arretone* 1235, *Athertone* 1255, *Areton* 1297. 'The farmstead or estate associated with a man called Ēadhere', from an Old English personal name with connective *-ing-* and *tūn*. The manor house itself dates back to 1639. The ancient St George's Church at Arreton, which incorporates some Anglo-Saxon architecture, is mentioned in the Domesday Book of 1086.

23

THE PLACE-NAMES OF THE ISLE OF WIGHT

Arreton Down (near Arreton). Recorded as *Aretone Downe* c.1540, from Old English *dūn* 'hill, down'. Its earlier name in medieval times was *Berdun* 1235-8, *Berdon* 1256, *Berton Downe* 1524, probably 'the down where barley is grown', with a first element Old English *bere* 'barley'.

Ashengrove (near Calbourne). Recorded as *Ashingrove* in 1630, that is 'the grove where ash-trees grow', from Old English *æscen* and *grāf*. Ashengrove is probably to be identified with a boundary point called *æscstede* ('the ash-tree place', from Old English *æsc* and *stede*) mentioned in the Saxon bounds of Calbourne (in a charter dated 826) and of Watchingwell (in a charter dated 968).

Ashey (north-west of Brading), **Ashey Down, East Ashey Manor Farm, West Ashey Farm.** *Æsces hege* 982 (in a 14th-century copy of a Saxon charter), *Assheshey* 1280, *Asshesheghe* 1351, *Ayshey* 1380. Probably 'the hedge or enclosure by the ash-tree', from Old English *æsc* (genitive case *æsces*) and *hege* or *hæg*. Alternatively 'the hedge or enclosure of a man called Æsc', with an Old English personal name as first element. In the Domesday Book of 1086 an estate called *Abedestone* ('the abbot's farm', from Old English *abbod* and *tūn*) is probably to be identified with Ashey: this description would refer to the fact that Ashey had earlier been in the possession of New Minster, Winchester before it was seized by the Conqueror after 1066.

Ashhill (near Atherfield). Not recorded before the 18th century (*Ahills* (sic) 1769, *Ashills* 1781), but self-explanatory and perhaps to be associated with Alice *atte Asshe* 1320, John *atte Nasche* 1327, '(living) at the ash-tree', from Old English *æsc* 'ash-tree' with Middle English *atte(n)* 'at the'.

Ashlake Farm (near Fishbourne). *Ashlake* 1862, named from a stream simply called *La Lake* in the 13th century, from Old English *lacu* 'a stream'.

Atherfield, Little, Atherfield Farm & Green, Atherfield Point (south of Shorwell). *Aderingefelda* 959 (in a copy from c.1300), *Avrefel, Egrafel* 1086 (Domesday Book), *Atherefeld* 1205, *Adherfeld* 1248, *Atherfeld* 1287. 'The open land of the family or followers of a

THE DICTIONARY

man called Ēadhere or Æthelhere', from an Old English personal name with -*inga*- and *feld*. The much reduced Domesday Book forms show the influence of Norman spelling on the English name. *Atherfield Farm* and *Atherfield Rocks & Point* are marked on Andrews's map of 1769.

Bachelors Farm (near Godshill). *Bachylers* 1552, *Bachilere grounde* 1576. A manorial name, from a local family called *Bacheler* mentioned in connection with Gatcombe in 1397.

Back of the Island, The. A name applied to that part of the Island lying between St Catherine's Point and The Needles. Alternatively 'the Back of Wight', the term does not seem to have been recorded at an early date.

Bagwich (near Godshill). *Abaginge* 1086 (Domesday Book), *Bagwich* c.1178, *Bagewich* 1198-1216, *Bagewyche* 1299, *Bagwygche* 1559. The second element is Old English wīc 'a dwelling, a specialized farm or building, a dairy farm'. The first element is more difficult. It may be the Old English masculine personal name Bacga, or a word **bagga* 'a bag' used either as a topographical term for a hill or as the name of some animal, possibly the badger. The Domesday Book spelling is corrupt but probably belongs here: the initial *A*- represents Old English *Æt* 'at'.

Barnsley Farm (2 miles north of Brading). *Benverdeslei, Benveslei* 1086 (Domesday Book), *Bernarddesle* 1203, *Barmardesle* 1351. 'The woodland clearing of a man called Beornfrith or Beornheard', from Old English lēah and an Old English personal name. The Domesday Book spelling suggests that the first element is Beornfrith, the later spellings point rather to Beornheard.

Barrack Shute (in Niton). This name recalls the site of a barracks in use in the early 19th century during the Napoleonic Wars. In the old dialect of Wight, the word *shute* (from Old English *scyte*) means 'a steep hill in a road or lane'.

25

THE PLACE-NAMES OF THE ISLE OF WIGHT

Bartlett's Farm (near Newchurch). Named from a local family called *Bartlett* mentioned in 16th- and 17th-century records for Ashey (e.g. Robert *Bartlett* 1560, Ranken *Bartlett* 1664).

Bartlett's Green Farm (2 miles north of Brading). Like the previous name, from a local family called *Bartlett*.

Barton (in Newport). First recorded as *Barton Village* 1862. Named from a row of houses built 1841-51 by a builder called *Barton*.

Barton Manor, Barton Wood (near Whippingham). *Burton* 1274, *Burtone* 1289, *Berton* 1392, *Burton alias Barton* 1438. Originally 'the fortified farmstead' or 'the farmstead near a fortification', from Old English *burh-tūn*. Later there was confusion with a quite different word, Old English *bere-tūn* 'a corn farm, an outlying grange or demesne farm'. Barton Manor is a Jacobean manor house, but it incorporates medieval lancet windows from a former Augustinian priory here, the Oratory or Priory of the Holy Trinity founded in 1275.

Barton's Corner (near Shalfleet). Named from a local family called *Barton*, of whom Richard *Barton* senior and junior (father and son) held copyhold farms on the east side of Barton's Corner from c.1600 to 1680. Another Bartons Corner near Binstead is thought to be named after members of the same family who settled there c.1710.

Bathingbourne (1½ miles north-east of Godshill). *Beaddingaburna* c.953 (in a 12th-century copy of a Saxon charter), *Bedingeborne* 1086 (Domesday Book), *Baddingeburne* 1235, *Bathyngbourne* 1346, *Bangborne* 1577. 'The stream of the family or followers of a man called *Beadda*', from an Old English personal name with *-inga-* and *burna*. The 1577 spelling reflects the local pronunciation of this name since the 16th century, so the modern spelling of the name is quite conservative!

Beacon Alley (near Godshill). No doubt a reference to the site of a beacon, perhaps on Bleak Down, one of many which once existed on the Island in medieval times and which would be lit to warn of impending invasion or other emergencies.

THE DICTIONARY

Beaper Farm (1½ miles north of Brading). *Beurepeyr* 1278, *Beaurepeyr* 1299, *Beawpere* 1502, *Biaper* 1769. 'Beautiful retreat', from Old French *beau* and *repaire*. One of the few Norman-French names on the Island, although this same name occurs in other parts of England, for example as Beaurepaire in Hampshire and Belper in Derbyshire.

Beckfield Cross (in Kingston). Named from *Beckfield Barn* 1769, but in the absence of earlier spellings the origin of *Beck-* must remain doubtful. Cross is used here in the sense 'cross-roads'.

Bedbury Lane (in Freshwater). Named from *Bydberu* 1418, *Bidborrow* 1608, which is probably from Old English *beorg* 'hill, mound, barrow' with an uncertain first element, possibly an Old English personal name *Bida or Bīeda.

Bembridge (near St Helens). *Bynnebrygg* 1316, *Bynbrygge* 1441, *Binbrigge* 1462, *Bembridge* 1775. '(The place lying) within the bridge', that is 'this side of the bridge', from Old English *binnan* and *brycg*. The name refers to the situation of Bembridge on a peninsula at the eastern extremity of the Island. In former times the course of the River Yar was a broad tidal creek as far south as Brading, and 'the Isle of Bembridge' (or *Binbridge Isle* as it is called on Speed's map of 1611) could only be reached by boat or by crossing the bridge at Yarbridge. Since, as Mr C. D. Webster points out, this bridge is known to have been built c.1300, the name Bembridge cannot predate its construction. The older name of Bembridge may have been *Orham*, since the present village is possibly the site of the Domesday Book manor of *Orham* (1086), 'the river-meadow or promontory by the shore', from Old English *ōra* and *hamm*.

Bembridge Down (near Bembridge). Recorded as *Binbridge downe* in 1583, *Bembridge Down* in 1769, but earlier called *Puttokesdone* in 1324, 'the down of the kite', from Old English *$*puttoc$* and *dūn*. The reference in 1324 is to the site of a beacon.

Bembridge Farm (near Bembridge). So named on Andrews's map of 1769.

THE PLACE-NAMES OF THE ISLE OF WIGHT

Bembridge Harbour (near Bembridge). Recently still referred to as Brading Harbour, a reminder that Brading was once a seaport when the course of the River Yar was a broad tidal creek. On Speed's map of 1611 it is called *S. Hellens haven*.

Bembridge Point (in Bembridge). First recorded on Andrews's map of 1769 as *Bambridge Point*.

Berryl (near Whitwell). *Berehulle* 1279, *Berhulle* 1280, *Berelle* 1445, *Berryl* 1781. 'The hill where barley is grown', from Old English *bere* and *hyll*.

Bierley (near Whitwell). *Berlay* 1341, *Beer ley* 1565. Probably 'the woodland clearing where barley is grown', from Old English *bere* and *lēah*.

Bigbury Farm (1 mile south of Newchurch). *Bikeberge* c.1222, *Bickeburgh* c.1240, *Bykebergh* 1284, *Bygbarowe* c.1540, *Bigbury* 1769. Probably 'the hill with a pointed ridge', from Old English **bica* and *beorg*. There was a grange of Quarr Abbey here in medieval times.

Billingham Manor (near Kingston). *Billigeham* 1189-1204, *Bilingham* 1235, *Belling(e)ham* 1248, *Bylyngham* 1280, *Billyngham* 1292. Probably 'the homestead or enclosure near to the ridge or hill', from Old English **bil(l)ing* and *hām* or *hamm*. The present manor house here dates back to the 17th century.

Binfield Farm (1 mile south of Whippingham). The present name is not on early record, but it was originally called *Claybrook* (as on Andrews's map of 1769) or *Claybrooke* (as in the 1851 Census). This is an old name, recorded as *Cleibroc* c.1200, *Cleybroc* 1266, that is 'the clayey brook', from Old English *clǣg* and *brōc*, originally referring to a small tributary of the River Medina.

Binnel Bay & Point (near Niton). *Binnel point* 1759, possibly to be associated with *Bynhille* 1299 which may mean 'the hill where beans are grown' from Old English *bēan* and *hyll*, or alternatively 'the place within the hill' from Old English *binnan* and *hyll*.

THE DICTIONARY

Binstead (medieval parish, near Ryde). *Benestede* 1086 (Domesday Book), *Benstede* 1225, *Bienstede* 1291, *Binsted* 1538. 'The place where beans are grown', from Old English *bēan* and *stede*. Binsted in Hampshire and Sussex are identical in origin. The beans in question would be both 'horse-beans' and 'broad-beans' – the latter were an essential element in the poor man's diet.

Birchfield House (south of Newport). Self-explanatory, a name given to the house by Henry Blake who built it c.1800 as his residence on land belonging to his father James Blake of Birchmore; see next name.

Birchmore Farm (near Rookley). *Berchemora* c.1200, *Byrchesmour* 1409, *Byrchemore* 1559, *Great & Little Birchmore* 1769. 'The moor or marshy ground where birch-trees grow', from Old English *bierce* and *mōr*.

Blackbridge Brook (near Havenstreet). Takes its name from an early forerunner of the bridge which crosses the brook just south-west of Havenstreet, recorded as *Blakbrigge* c.1216, *Blakebrigge* c.1224, *Blakebrygge* 1444, *Blackbrydge* c.1540, *Black Bridge* 1769, 'the black or dark-coloured bridge', from Old English *blæc* and *brycg*. The document dated c.1216 is a grant giving Quarr Abbey freedom to construct a bridge over the water at *Blakbrigge*.

Blackgang, Blackgang Chine (near Chale). First recorded in 1781, and meaning 'the dark path or track' from Old English *blæc* and *gang*, with reference to the path along the bottom of the Chine. A fitting name for a path reputed to have been used for smuggling, although the interpretation sometimes suggested, that the name refers to a 'black gang' of smugglers, is simply misleading! The word *chine* is from Old English *cinu* 'a fissure, a ravine', and the ravine to which it refers gave name at a much earlier date to the village of Chale.

Blacklands Farm (east of Newport). *la Blakelond* c.1215, *la Blakelande* 1227, *Blakelond* 1258, *Blackelondes* 1524, *Blackland* 1769. 'The cultivated land with black or dark-coloured soil', from Old English *blæc* and *land*. The name was originally singular, the plural *-s* first appearing in the 16th century.

29

THE PLACE-NAMES OF THE ISLE OF WIGHT

Black Pan (near Sandown). *Bochepone* 1086 (Domesday Book), *Blakepenn* c.1200, *Blakepanne* 1235, *Blakpanne* 1428, *Black Pann* 1769. 'The black or dark-coloured pen or fold for animals', from Old English *blæc* and *penn*. The Domesday Book spelling of this name is rather erratic.

Black Rock Ledge (in Bembridge). Appears as *Blacke Rocke* on a map of 1550 in the British Library, and as *Black rock* on a map of 1591, self-explanatory. There is another Black Rock in Freshwater.

Blackwater (1 mile south of Newport). Recorded thus from 1548, 'the dark-coloured stream', from Old English *blæc* and *wæter*. The name may have originally referred to the stream which runs into the River Medina here. A century ago the mill at Blackwater was known as *Huffingford Mill*, this being an ancient name recorded as *Ovingefort* or *Huncheford* in the Domesday Book of 1086, later as *Huvingeford* 1289, *Hofyngeford* c.1300. Its probable meaning is 'the ford of the people living by the hood-shaped hill', from Old English *hūfe* with *-inga-* and *ford*.

Blakes (near Brighstone). Recorded thus on Andrews's map of 1769, named from the ancestors of the *Blake* family of Birchfield and Birchmore, here c.1550-1650.

Blanket Copse (near Wootton). Named from a Richard *Blankett* who held a small tenement in Alverstone (south-east of Whippingham) in the early 17th century.

Bleak Down (near Godshill). *La Blakedon* c.1190 (in a 14th-century copy), *Blickedun* 1203, *Blikedon* c.1280, *Blekedowne* 1576, *Black Down* 1769. Probably 'the hill or down bare of vegetation', from Old English *blǣc* and *dūn*.

Bloodstone Copse (near Ashey). Near a spring named *Bloodstone Well*, apparently so called from the blood-red incrustation on some of the stones in its bed.

Bobberstone Farm (near Godshill). *Boberstone* 1459, *Boverstone* 1556, *Bouestone* 1564, *Bobberston* 1670. The early spellings are

THE DICTIONARY

ambiguous, but possibly a name containing Old English *tūn* 'manor, estate' with the surname *Bob(b)ere* of some early owner.

Bohemia Corner (1 mile north-west of Godshill). Named from a tenement at Roud referred to as *Bohemia* in a deed dated 1730 and on Taylor's map of 1759. Transferred names such as this from other parts of the world were often given to places considered isolated or remote. There is another place called Bohemia in Redlynch, Wiltshire.

Bonchurch (medieval parish, near Ventnor), **Upper Bonchurch**. *Bonecerce* 1086 (Domesday Book), *Bonechurch* c.1270, *Bonechirch* 1283, *Bonecherche* 1291, *St Boniface alias Bonchurch* 1528. Probably 'the church of *Bona', from Old English *cirice* and an Old English personal name which may be a short-form of the Latin name *Bonifatius* (i.e. *Boniface*), the saint to whom the church here is dedicated. St Boniface, born in Devon c.675, became chiefly renowned for taking the Christian gospel to the heathen tribes of Germany, but may have been specially venerated here during the Anglo-Saxon period; see also nearby St Boniface Down which is so named from at least as early as the 13th century. This traditional explanation of the name has recently been convincingly defended by Professor Richard Coates. The 'old church' of St Boniface at Bonchurch is early Norman in date, but may have been built on the site of the original Saxon church referred to in the name.

Borthwood Farm & Copse (near Newchurch). *Bordovrde* 1086 (Domesday Book), *Bordwode* c.1222, *Bordewode* 1333, *Brodewode* 1384, *Lower & Upper Borthwood* 1769. Probably 'the wood where boards or planks are obtained', from Old English *bord* and *wudu*. Alternatively the word *bord* may be used in the sense 'border', referring to the situation of this former forest on the boundary between Brading and Newchurch. *Sandham Castle* (see Sandown) was built of timber from the *Forest of Bordwood* in the time of Henry VIII.

Bouldnor, Bouldnor Cliff (near Thorley). *Boulner* c.1150, *Bolenoura* 1181, *Bulner* 1202, *Bolner* 1299, *Bulenore* 1345, *East & West Bouldner* 1769. Literally 'the shore of the bull', from Old

THE PLACE-NAMES OF THE ISLE OF WIGHT

English *bula (genitive case *bulan) and ōra. The name may refer to the grazing of bulls here. Alternatively the outline of Bouldnor Cliff, which rises steeply to a height of 200 feet, might have been thought to resemble the shape of a bull, giving a meaning 'shore by a cliff called The Bull'. See Cowes for a similar animal shape-name used of a topographical feature.

Bowcombe (1 mile south-west of Carisbrooke). *Bovecome, Bouecome* 1086 (Domesday Book), *Boecombe* 1141-3, *Bouecumba* 1185, *Bouecombe* 1255, *Bowcombe* 1299, *Buccomb* 1635. Possibly 'the valley belonging to a man called Bofa', from Old English *cumb* and an Old English personal name. Alternatively '(the place) above the valley', from Old English *bufan* and *cumb*. In this case the name would originally have applied to Bowcombe Down (see next entry), later transferred to the valley itself and the settlement there. At the time of Domesday Book, Bowcombe was the name of a Hundred (the principal one on the Island), and the meetings of the Hundred must have been held here, either on the down or in the valley. The name Bowcombe is sometimes interpreted as 'fair valley' from the French word *beau*, but this is quite incorrect.

Bowcombe Down (near Bowcombe). *la Dune* late 13th century, *la Done* 1411, *Boucombe Downe* 1608, *Buccomb Down* 1769. 'The hill or down at Bowcombe', from Old English *dūn*. An important pagan Jutish or Saxon cemetery has been discovered here, with both cremation and inhumation burials.

Brading (medieval parish, north-east of Sandown). *Brerdinges* 683 (in a 14th-century copy of a Saxon charter), *Berardinz* 1086 (Domesday Book), *Brardinge* 1218, *Brerdinge* 1235, *Bradyng* 1507. '(The settlement of) the dwellers on the hill-side', from Old English *brerd* and *-ingas*. The word *brerd* 'hill-side, ridge' refers to Brading Down, on the eastern slopes of which Brading is situated. Brading is an ancient name of great interest, for it is the only one of the 'folk-name' type on the Island: that is, it originally referred to a tribe or family of settlers, later (before Domesday Book) becoming the name of the settlement itself. The meaning 'broad meadow' sometimes given to Brading is quite incorrect.

THE DICTIONARY

Brading Down (near Brading). So called on Andrews's map of 1769.

Brading Harbour. The older name for what is now usually called Bembridge Harbour. Brading was once a seaport before the broad tidal creek of the River Yar was drained in the late 19th century, and the remains of a quay are still visible.

Brambles Chine (near Totland). Named from a place called *Brambles* recorded on Andrews's map of 1769, and perhaps to be associated with *Bramblehill* 1608. So called from Lazarus *Bramble*, a master mariner from Yarmouth who held this land in 1648. The word *chine* is from Old English *cinu* 'a fissure, a ravine'.

Branstone (1 mile south of Newchurch). *Brandestone* 1086 (Domesday Book), *Brondestone* c.1240, *Braundeston* 1289, *Brondeston* 1385, *Brenston* 1769. 'The farmstead or estate belonging to a man called Brandr', from Old English *tūn* and an Old Scandinavian personal name. Brandr (like the Sveinn who gave name to Swainston) was almost certainly of Viking or Norman stock.

Briddlesford Lodge, Great Briddlesford Farm (1 mile south of Wootton Bridge). *Breilesforde* 1086 (Domesday Book), *Bridlesford* 1167, *Bridleford* 1179, *Brydelesford* 1280, *Great & Little Briddlesford* 1769. 'The bridle ford', that is 'the deep ford only passable by a horse or on horseback', from Old English *brigdels* or *brīdels* and *ford*.

Bridgecourt (near Godshill). *Bryggecourt* 1465, *Bridge court* 1611. 'The large house or manor at Bridge' (see next name), from Middle English *court*. The present house here dates back to the early 17th century.

Bridge Farm (near Godshill). *la Brige* 1235, *la Brigge* 1255, *la Brugge* 1280, *Brygge* 1423. '(The place at) the bridge', from Old English *brycg*, referring to a former bridge across the River Yar. *Bridge Mill* is marked on Andrews's map of 1769.

Brighstone (medieval parish, near Shorwell). ?*Weristetone* (sic) 1086 (Domesday Book), *Brihtwiston* 1212, *Brichtestone* 1257, *Brightestone*

THE PLACE-NAMES OF THE ISLE OF WIGHT

1276, *Brixton* 1399, *Brighstone* 1431, *Brykston* 1550. 'The farmstead or estate belonging to a man called Beorhtwīg', from Old English *tūn* and an Old English personal name. If the Domesday spelling belongs here, which is probable, the Norman scribe must have written *Wer-* instead of *Ber-*. The 14th-century spelling *Brixton* represents the local pronunciation of the name still heard. Although Brighstone was included in a grant of land at Calbourne by King Ecgbert of Wessex to the see of Winchester in 826, the name cannot possibly mean 'Ecgbert's estate' as is sometimes claimed.

Brighstone Bay, Down & Forest (near Brighstone). Recorded as *Brixton Bay, Brixton Down* 1769, *Brixton Down gate* 1596.

Brook (medieval parish, near Mottistone). *Broc* 1086 (Domesday Book), *manerio del Broc* c.1194, *Broke* c.1200, *la Broke* 1276, *Brouke* 1327, *Brooke* 1348. '(The place at) the brook', from Old English *brōc*, referring to the small stream which flows into the sea at Brook Bay. In the spelling dated c.1194, *del* represents 'of the'.

Brook Bay & Chine, Brook Down & House, Brookgreen, Brook Hill (all in Brook). *Brook Chine, Brook Green, Brook House* are all so named on Andrews's map of 1769, *Brook Down* appears on Worsley's map of 1781. The earlier name of Brook Bay was *Hanemouth* 'the stony or rocky river mouth' from Old English **hānen* and *mūth*, this apparently giving name to the nearby Hanover Point.

Buckbury (east of Newport). *Buggebury* 1333, *Bukkebury* 1410, *Bokkebury* 1412, *Bucbury* 1557. Probably 'the fortified place of a man called Bucca', from Old English *burh* (dative *byrig*) and an Old English personal name.

Bucks Farm (near Kingston). No doubt named from a family called *Buck* who also gave their name to *Bucks Barn, Bucks Common* on Andrews's map of 1769, and *Bucks Heath* on Worsley's map of 1781. Mr C. D. Webster notes that the only early reference to a family of this name in the Kingston area is to John *Bukke*, rector of Kingston 1364-74.

THE DICTIONARY

Budbridge Manor, Great, & Little Budbridge Farm (near Godshill). *Butebrigge* 1235, *Buttebrigge* c.1248, *Botebrigg* 1292, *Buttebrigge* 1299, *Budbridge* 1559, *Great & Little Butbridge* 1769. Possibly 'the bridge belonging to a man called *Butta', from Old English *brycg* and an Old English personal name. Alternatively the first element may be an Old English word **butt* 'tree-trunk, log', in which case the meaning would be 'the bridge made of tree-trunks or logs'. The manor house here is Jacobean.

Buddle (in Niton). *Buddle or Buddel* 1580, *Buddell place* 1608, *Boddle* 1769. 'The dwelling-place', from Old English *bōthl*. Places with this name in Hampshire and Somerset have the same origin.

Bullen House (near Nettlestone). Recorded on Taylor's map of 1759 as *Bullen*, and to be associated with *Little Bullen* 1702 and with fields called *Bullens* in 1842, but earlier spellings are needed to explain the name's origin.

Bull Ring (in Brading). The same name occurs in Niton as the name of a field. Both are a reminder that the cruel sport of bull-baiting once took place here and elsewhere in earlier times. Indeed in the *Assize for Butchers* (1636) we are informed 'that Butchers may not kill or sell any bull or bulls unbaiten'.

Bull Rocks (off Mottistone). So named on Taylor's map of 1759, but called *Bullplace Point* on a chart of 1720. Named from the local family called *Bull* who lived at Pitt Place (in Mottistone) and Bull Place (in Brook) for many generations.

Bulls Wood (2 miles north-east of Calbourne). Named from the local family called *Bull* who owned Watchingwell in the 17th and 18th century.

Bunts Hill Farm (near Locksgreen). Marked as *Burnt Hill* on Andrews's map of 1769, but probably to be associated with *Bunse* 1608 and no doubt named from the family called *Bunt* who also gave their name to *Bunts House* 1769 (marked on Andrews's map near Vittlefields).

THE PLACE-NAMES OF THE ISLE OF WIGHT

Burnt House (south-east of Newport). Although self-explanatory, the name has a particularly gruesome history, for as Mr C. D. Webster points out, this is said to be the house where Michael Mory murdered his grandson James Dove in 1736 and which he then set on fire to cover his tracks.

Burnt House (near Alverstone). First recorded as *Barnd Ho* on Andrews's map of 1769, but identical in origin with the previous name.

Burnt Wood (near Porchfield). Recorded as *Burntwood* in a 1630 survey and with its present spelling on Andrews's map of 1769. Self-explanatory.

Calbourne (medieval parish, north of Brighstone). *Cawelburnan* 826 (in a 12th-century copy of a Saxon charter), *Cavborne* 1086 (Domesday Book), *Cauelburn* 1181, *Calburna* 1232, *Caulburne* 1247. Probably 'the stream where cole or cabbage grows', from Old English *cawel* and *burna*; the reference would no doubt be to sea-cabbage or sea-kale. Alternatively the first element may be an ancient Celtic river-name *Cawel* of uncertain meaning but identical with the River Cale (earlier also *Cawel*) in Somerset. In either case the name Calbourne originally denoted the stream here (still known as Caul Bourne) before it was transferred to the settlement. The 13th-century All Saints' Church at Calbourne stands on the site of an earlier church mentioned in the Domesday Book of 1086.

Callibury or Gallibury Hump (near Calbourne). See under G-.

Carisbrooke (medieval parish, south-west of Newport). *Caresbroc, Caresbroke, Karesbrok, Karisbroch* 12th century, *Carisbrok* 1324, *Casebroke* 1393. Possibly 'the brook called Cary', from Old English *brōc* and a lost Celtic river-name identical with the River Cary (perhaps meaning 'pleasant stream') in Somerset. If this interpretation is correct, *Cary* will have been the ancient original name of what is now Lukely Brook. An even earlier name for Carisbrooke itself may have been *Wihtwaraburh* 'the stronghold of the people of Wight', from Old English *-ware* and *burh*, although this always appears in early (6th-century) sources as *Wihtgaraburh*

THE DICTIONARY

probably through an assumed association with Wihtgār, a Jutish chieftain mentioned in the Anglo-Saxon Chronicle. Although much of the present castle here dates mainly from the Tudor period, the earlier Norman castle (of which the keep remains) was almost certainly erected on the foundations of a more ancient defensive fortress (to which Old English *burh* could have referred); indeed there are still traces of a small Roman fort near the castle entrance.

Carpenters Farm (near St Helens). Recorded as *Carpenters* in 1552. Named from the local *Carpenter* family; John *Carpenter* was tenant here in 1450.

Cassys (near Kingston). Recorded as *Cawses* 1786. A manorial name, indicating lands here once owned by the local family called *Cause* (a John *Cawse* or *Cause* is mentioned in the 1664-5 Hearth Tax returns for South Shorwell).

Castle Haven (in Niton). Named from *Old Castle* marked on Andrews's map of 1769.

Castle Hill (in Mottistone). The 'castle' refers to a hill-top bank and ditch enclosure here that may be Iron Age in date.

Castlehold (now Upper High Street in Newport). *Castle hold* 1611, *St Nicholas or Castlehold* 1664, *Castlehold* 1669. From Middle English *holde* in the sense 'possession, tenure', so called from its having originally denoted the '13½ places of land' in Newport which Isabella de Fortibus, Lady of Wight in the 13th century, reserved for the use of the Castle of Carisbrooke. The 1664 form refers to the fact that Castlehold was a detached part of the parish of St Nicholas, Carisbrooke.

Caul Bourne. See Calbourne, to which place this stream gave its name.

Centurion's Copse (near Brading). Although some Roman pottery and tiles were actually discovered here in 1840, this name is really only a corruption of *St Urian's Copse*, named from a former chapel dedicated to St Urian or Eurien! The chapel is first mentioned in a document of 1305, and a piece of ground called *le Chapelfeld*, named from the chapel, is also recorded from the early 14th century.

Chale (medieval parish, west of Niton). *Cela* 1086 (Domesday Book), *Chale* 1114, 1167, *Chele* 1181, c.1290. '(Place at) the gorge or ravine', from Old English *ceole*. This word, literally meaning 'a throat', was sometimes used in this transferred sense in place-names, here no doubt referring originally to the famous ravine in the cliffs, nearly 400 feet deep, now known as Blackgang Chine.

Chale Bay & Chale Green (near Chale). The former is first recorded on a map of 1550; according to the *Shell Guide*, it used to be called 'the Bay of Death' because the coast here was so notoriously dangerous to shipping. An earlier name for Chale Green seems to have been Stroud Green (spelt *Stroad Green* on Andrews's map of 1769), named from *Stroude* 1345, this representing Old English *strōd* 'marshy land overgrown with brushwood'.

Champion Farm (near Rookley). Recorded as *Champion* from the 16th century, so called from a local family of this name.

Chessell Farm, Little Chessell (near Shalcombe). *Chestelon* 1193-1217, *Chesthull* 1228, *Chestull* 1278, *Cheshulle* 1280, *Chestelle* 1301, *(Little) Chestle* 1769. Probably 'hill where chests or coffins were found', from Old English *cest* and *hyll*, with reference no doubt to the important pagan Jutish cemetery, in use during the 6th century, discovered on Chessell Down. In the earliest spelling, the final *-(l)on* may represent Old English *lanu* 'lane' or *land* 'land' or an Old French diminutive suffix *-on*.

Cheverton Down & Farm (near Shorwell). *Cevredone* 1086 (Domesday Book), *Cheuerdone* 1235, *Chiverdon* 1281, *Chyverdone* 1346, *Chevertone* 1557. 'The hill or down infested with chafers or beetles', from Old English *ceafor* and *dūn*. The word *down* (the modern descendant of Old English *dūn*) was only added once again to the name when the spelling of the final element was changed from *-don* to *-ton* in the 16th century, long after the original significance of the name had been forgotten.

THE DICTIONARY

Cheverton Farm (near Shanklin). *Chevertons* 16th century, *Chiverton* 1769, *Cheverton* 1793. Probably a manorial name, indicating lands here once owned by a family called *Cheverton* who took their name from Cheverton near Shorwell.

Chillerton, Chillerton Down & Farm (near Gatcombe). *Celertune* 1086 (Domesday Book), *Chelertona* 1189-1204, *Cheliertone* 1279, *Chelyerton* 1327, *Chillerton Common, Down, Farm & Street* 1769. Probably 'enclosed farmstead in a valley', from Old English *ceole, geard* 'yard or enclosure' and *tūn*. Alternatively the name may mean 'farmstead belonging to a man called Cēolheard', with an Old English personal name as first element. The Down, first recorded on Worsley's map of 1781, is the site of an Iron Age hill fort, the only definite one of its type found on the Island.

Chillingwood Farm (1 mile south of Havenstreet). *Ceollingwuda* 982 (in the 14th-century Hyde Cartulary), *Chelingewod* c.1218, *Chellingewode* c.1240, *Chelingewode* 1279, *Chillingwode* 1289. Probably 'wood at the valley place or stream', from Old English *ceole* (or **ceolle*) with *-ing* and *wudu*. Alternatively the first element may be an Old English masculine personal name *Ceolla*, giving a meaning 'wood at Ceolla's place' (with *-ing*), or 'wood of the family or followers of a man called Ceolla' (with *-inga-*).

Chilton Chine, Chilton Farm (near Brighstone). *Celatune* 1086 (Domesday Book), *Cheltona* 1173, *Cheletuna* c.1192, *Cheleton* 1289, *Chilton* 1306. Probably 'the farmstead or estate near the gorge or deep valley', from Old English *ceole* and *tūn*, originally with reference to the chine here. However it is formally possible for the name to mean 'farmstead or estate belonging to a man called Cēola', from an Old English personal name. *Chilton Chine* is marked on Andrews's map of 1769.

Churchills Farm (near Shalcombe). *Cherchulle* 1295, *Cherchehelle* 1299, *Churchills* 1769. Apparently 'hill belonging to the church (at Shalfleet)', from Old English *cirice* and *hyll*. It is to be noted that the final *-s*, giving this the appearance of a manorial name, is relatively recent.

THE PLACE-NAMES OF THE ISLE OF WIGHT

Church Litten (in Newport). The dialect word *litten* is from Old English *līc-tūn* 'burial ground'. This land was first licensed as a graveyard in 1582, during the reign of Elizabeth I.

Clamerkin, Clamerkin Lake (near Newtown). This curious and unusual name first appears in the records as *Clamerken* on Andrews's map of 1769. It is manorial in origin, as is clear from a rental of 1507 which refers to the holding as 'late in the occupation of Thomas *Clamorgan*', no doubt from an illegitimate line of the great family of this name who owned large estates on the Island in the 13th and 14th centuries. The word *lake* is from Old English *lacu* 'a stream', as in the place-name Lake itself.

Clatterford (in Carisbrooke). *Claterford* c.1150, *Clatreford* c.1200, *Claterford* 1289, *Clateruorde* 1331, *Clatterford* 1708. 'The ford with loose stones or pebbles', from an Old English **clater* and *ford*. The same name occurs in Essex. The ford was across Lukely Brook.

Cliff End (near Colwell Bay). Self-explanatory, first recorded as *Clevesend* 1720, *Cliffs End* 1769.

Cliff Farm (near Northwood). Named from *le Cliffe* 1608, 'the cliff' from Old English *clif*.

Cockleton (in Northwood). *Cocheltone* 1255, *Cokeltone* 1299, *Cokkeltone* 1327, *Cockleton* 1708. Probably 'the farmstead where cockle grows', from Old English *coccel* 'corncockle, a cornfield weed' and *tūn*.

Coleman's Farm (near Locksgreen). On record as *Colmans* in 1559, no doubt a manorial name indicating land originally held by a family called *Col(e)man*.

Colwell Bay (near Totland). So called on Andrews's map of 1769, and named from *Colewhelle* 1417, *Collwell* 1608, *Colwell* 1720. This means 'the cool spring', from Old English *cōl* and *wella*, and no doubt refers to one of the springs issuing from the cliffs at Colwell Bay.

THE DICTIONARY

Combley Farm, Combley Great Wood (near Arreton). *Combelia* 1228-38, *grange of Comblye* 1249, *Cumbele* 1255, *Comblie* 1279, *(grange of) Coumley* 1534, *Combley (Wood)* 1769. 'The wood or woodland clearing in a valley', from Old English *cumb* and *lēah*. In medieval times Combley was the largest grange of Quarr Abbey, a *grange* being 'an outlying farm where crops are stored'.

Combtonfield (near Atherfield). So called on Andrews's map of 1769, and named from a family called *Compton* who had lands here as early as the 13th century (and who came from Compton in Freshwater).

Compton Bay, Chine, Down & Farm (near Freshwater). *Cantune* 1086 (Domesday Book), *Cumpton* 1155-61, *Cumptune* late 12th century, *Comptona* 1218, *Comptone* 1248. 'The farmstead or estate in a valley', from Old English *cumb* and *tūn*. Compton Bay is so named on a map of 1550, Compton Chine is first shown on Andrews's map of 1769, and Compton Down first appears as *Comptons Downe* in 1518. Compton Grange (simply *Grange* on Andrews's map of 1769) is probably the site of a medieval grange belonging to Quarr Abbey.

Cook's Castle (near Wroxall). A ruin of uncertain date, first recorded with its present name on Worsley's map of 1781 and no doubt named from a local family called *Cook*. It is possibly to be identified with a castle mentioned in 16th-century documents as *Baynardes Castell*, named from an earlier family called *Baynard*.

Coombe Farm (near Brighstone). *Cumbe* 1251, *la Cumbe* 1252, *the Combe* 1507, *Coombe* 1769. 'The valley', from Old English *cumb*. This place is to be identified with *Seutecome* in 1086 (Domesday Book), later *Shutecumbe* 1254, *Shetecombe* 1299. This means 'valley near Shate', with reference to another place situated in the same valley; see Shate. Coombe Tower was the site of a beacon in medieval times, referred to as *la Wyrde* in 1252 and 1324, from Old English **wierde* 'a watch, a look-out'.

Coppin's Bridge (in Newport). So called on Andrews's map of 1769, just to the north of *Coppin's Mill*. Named from a local family called *Copping* mentioned in 16th-century documents. The bridge was called *Godsbridge* in the 16th and early 17th century. At an even earlier date, the river-crossing here was called *Durneford* as in c.1258, 'the hidden or secret ford', from Old English *dierne* and *ford*.

Corfheath Firs (1 mile east of Newtown). So named because this represents the portion of *Heathfield Common* granted to *Corfe Farm* near Shalfleet (recorded as *Carf* on Andrews's map of 1769) when the common was divided up and enclosed in 1583. The first element is Old English **corf* 'a cutting, a gap or pass' as in the following name. The final part of the name probably represents an original *furze*.

Corve Farm (near Kingston). *la Corve* late 13th century, *Corue* 1428, *Corve* 1659. 'The cutting, the gap or pass', from Old English **corf*, with the French definite article in the earliest form. The same word is found in Corfe Castle and Corfe Mullen in Dorset, as well as in the previous name.

Cowes, East Cowes (4 miles north of Newport). Originally named from two sandbanks off the mouth of the River Medina called *Estcowe* and *Westcowe* in 1413, 'the east and west cow', from their fancied resemblance to animals: it is not at all unusual for coastal and offshore features like sandbanks and rocks to be named in this way (other local examples include Horse Ledge near Shanklin, Cow Ledge near Atherfield Point, and Bouldnor Cliff near Thorley). When, in about 1539, Henry VIII had two blockhouses or forts built to defend the coast against the French and Spanish, they in turn came to be called *the Est Cow* and *the West Cow* as recorded in *The Itinerary of John Leland* (1535-43); see Cowes Castle and Old Castle Point. Finally the plural name 'The Cow(e)s' came to be transferred to the settlements themselves on either side of the river estuary, giving the modern names *East Cowes* and *West Cowes* appearing on Andrews's map of 1769. An older name for Cowes seems to have been *Shamelord*, recorded from the 13th century and still surviving in the name Shamblers Copse: this is to be derived from Old English *sceamol* 'shelf, ledge' and *ord* 'point, spit of land'.

Cowes Castle (in West Cowes). So called on Andrews's map of 1769. Now the headquarters of the famous Royal Yacht Squadron Club, this mainly 18th-19th-century building incorporates the battery of the original fort built here in the time of Henry VIII (about 1539) to defend the Island against attack from the French and Spanish. The fort in question was once called *the West Cow* from its situation on the west side of the Medina estuary; see Cowes.

Cowes Roads (off Cowes). Recorded as *the roads called the Esturly or the Westerly Cowe* in 1539, from the word *road* in the old sense 'sheltered water where ships may ride at anchor'.

Cranmore (near Shalfleet). *Cranemore* 1235, *Cranmores* 1559, *Cranmore* 1781. 'The marshy ground frequented by cranes or herons', from Old English *cran* and *mōr*. The *mōr* is probably the one mentioned in a Saxon charter of the 10th century describing the bounds of nearby Ningwood, which proceed *to thæs mores heafde* 'to the head of the moor or marshland'.

Cridmore (near Chillerton). *Cruddemore* c.1286, *Crudmore* 1299, *Crodemor* 1305, *Crudemore* 1337, *Cridmore* 1708. 'The marshy ground overgrown with weeds or other vegetation', from Old English **crȳde* and *mōr*. The place is situated on low-lying land by the River Medina.

Crockers Farm (near Northwood). Recorded as *Crockers* in 1673 and on Andrews's map of 1769. Named from the word *crokkere* 'potmaker' as in the next name, although here probably used as the surname of a local family rather than as an occupational term.

Crocker Street (in Newport). Recorded as *Crockerestret* in the 14th century, 'street of the potmakers', from Middle English *crokkere* 'a maker of crocks or pots, a potter'.

Cross Lane (in Newport). Recorded as *the crosse lane* in 1668, meaning 'the lane that crosses from one road to another'.

Culver Cliff & Down (north-east of Sandown). The former is first recorded as *Culver Cleues* on a map of 1550 in the British Library, then as *Couluer clyffes* 1591, *Culver Cliff* 1700. 'The cliff(s) and down frequented by doves or pigeons', from Old English *culfre, clif*, and *dūn*. An alternative derivation sometimes suggested, from Old English *cofa* 'a cove', is incorrect.

Dallimores (near Whippingham). A manorial name from a local family called *Dallimore*; a John *Dallamore* or *Dalimoore* appears in the 1664-5 Hearth Tax returns for Northwood.

Deacons (near Ashey). Named from a local family called *Deacon*, of whom William *Deacon* held this tenement from the manor of Ashey in 1560 at a rent of 26 shillings. It was originally called *Twelve Pooks* from the dialect word *pook* 'large heap or small rick of hay or corn'.

Deadman's Brook (east of Newport). The modern name for the brook that gave name to Lynn Farm, and no doubt to be interpreted literally as a stream in which a dead body was once found.

Dean Farm (near St Lawrence). Recorded as *atte Dane* 1327, *atte Denne* 1378, *Dane* 1550, *Dean* 1769. From Old English *denu* 'a valley', which aptly describes its situation. The 14th-century spellings, occurring as the surnames of those living here, mean 'at the valley'.

Debourne (in West Cowes). *Debburna* 12th century (in a 14th-century copy), *Depeburne* 1255, *Debeburne* 1279, *Debbourne* 1333. Apparently 'the deep stream', from Old English *dēop* and *burna*, although there is no stream here now.

Devil's Chimney (near Ventnor). An evocative name for a narrow fissure between the rocks of the Upper Landslip. Curious and mysterious natural features were often thought to be the work of the devil or to be the haunt of evil spirits, but the same superstitious beliefs could be applied to ancient earthworks: see the following name.

Devil's Punchbowl (on Nunwell Down near Brading). The superstitious name given to a Bronze Age bowl barrow; see previous name.

THE DICTIONARY

Dodnor House (near Parkhurst). *Doddenorde* c.1195, *Dodenore* 1255, *Dodenorthe* 1297, *Doddenord* 1301, *Doddenorde* c.1330, *Dodner* 1769. 'The point or spit of land belonging to a man called Dodda', from an Old English personal name (genitive case *-an*) and *ord*. Although the name is almost certainly of pre-Conquest origin, the descendant of the Saxon *Dodda* was still here in the 12th century, for in c.1195 (Godshouse Cartulary) it is described as 'the virgate of land at *Doddenorde* which William *Dodde* held'.

Dolcoppice (2 miles south-west of Godshill). *terra Willelmi Dolecope* 13th century, *Dolcoppys* 1409, *Dolcoppes* 1430, *Doulecopse* 1588, *Dolcoppice* 1769. The first reference (in Latin) means 'land of William Dolecope', and this is therefore a place-name of the manorial type denoting an estate held by this family, mentioned several times in local records from the end of the 13th century. The modern form is a good example of the working of 'popular etymology': the nickname surname *Dolecope* (meaning 'dole-cup') in its possessive form *Dolecope's* has been falsely interpreted as a place-name containing the word *coppice*.

Doreshill Farm (2 miles east of Newport). A manorial name denoting lands held here at some date by the local family called *Dore*, mentioned in medieval records from the 13th century. In a Quarr Abbey charter dated c.1220 there is mention of a 'messuage once held by Robert *Dure*' (in Brading).

Downcourt (near St Catherine's Down). *Done, Ladone* 1086 (Domesday Book), *atte Doune* 1392, *Downecourt* 1445, *Dounecourt* 1446. Originally simply 'the hill or down', from Old English *dūn* (with reference to St Catherine's Down), later with the addition of Middle English *court* 'large house, manor'. In one of the Domesday Book spellings, *La-* represents the French definite article, whilst the 14th-century surname form *atte Doune* means '(living) at the hill or down'.

Downend (near Arreton). Self-explanatory, from its situation at the end of Arreton Down.

THE PLACE-NAMES OF THE ISLE OF WIGHT

Drapers (in Brighstone). Recorded thus from 1793, and named from a local family called *Draper* who were tenants here in the early 17th century.

Dungewood Farm (near Shorwell). *Dunniorde* 1086 (Domesday Book), *Donnyngeworth* 1327, *Dunnyngeworthe* 1379, *Dungewood* 1769. 'The enclosed farmstead of the family or followers of a man called Dunna', from an Old English personal name with *-inga-* and *worth*. Alternatively, if the medial syllable represents singular Old English *-ing*, 'the enclosed farmstead at the place belonging to Dunna'.

Dunnose (near Bonchurch). *Donnose* 1544, *Dounnose* 1550, *Donnesse* 1595, *Dunnose* 1769. 'The downland promontory or headland', from Old English *dūn* and *nose*.

Dunsbury (in Brook). Not recorded before the 16th century (*Donesbye* 1563, *Dunsbury* 1639, *Dunsberry Farm* 1780), but nevertheless possibly an early name, 'the fortified place of a man called Dunn', from Old English *burh* (dative case *byrig*) and an Old English personal name. There is mention of a separate holding *Donsbrooke* (besides *Donesbye*) in the 1563 Court Roll, this being presumably named from the brook (Old English *brōc*) belonging to the same man.

Durrants (1 mile south-east of Newton). *Durrandes* 1507, *Dorans* 1559. Apparently a manorial name, indicating earlier ownership of lands here by a family called *Durrand* or *Durrant*.

Durton Farm (1 mile north-west of Arreton). *Drodintone* 1086 (Domesday Book), *Drutitone* 1235, *Drotton* 1355, *Durton* 1769. Probably 'the farmstead or estate associated with a man called *Drūt*', from an Old English personal name with connective *-ing-* and Old English *tūn*.

Duver, The (in St Helens). This name, for the spit of land leading from the ruined tower of St Helen's Church and jutting out into Bembridge Harbour, is first recorded as *Dover* on Worsley's map of 1781. It represents a dialect word *dover* (from a French word *douvre*)

46

THE DICTIONARY

probably referring to some shoreline feature, either 'ridge of sand or stones' or 'salt-marsh channel'.

Duxmore Farm, Little Duxmore (1½ miles north of Newchurch). Recorded as *Duxmore* and *Duxmore Fm* on Andrews's map of 1769, and probably to be associated with *Dusmurrs (meade)* 1608. Earlier spellings are needed for an explanation to be possible. The old name of Duxmore seems to have been *Kyngeswelle* (so called in c.1258), 'the king's spring or stream', from Old English *cyning* and *wella*.

Eades Farm (near Newbridge). *Heeges* 1769, *Eaddses* 1812. A manorial name, indicating lands here held by the *Edes* family, although the first spelling is corrupt.

East Afton (near Freshwater), see Afton.

East Cliff (at Bembridge). No doubt a relatively modern name, with the development of Bembridge as a resort. There is also an East Cliff at Shanklin.

East Gate Barn (near Newbridge). Self-explanatory.

Easton (in Freshwater). *Estetune* 1244, *Estone* 1417, *Eston* 1608, *Easton* 1781. 'The eastern farmstead or estate', from Old English $\bar{e}ast$ and $t\bar{u}n$, originally named in relation to Middleton, Norton and Weston Manor (all originally in Freshwater parish).

Eddington (in St Helens), see St Helens.

Egypt Point (in West Cowes). First recorded as *Egypt Clift* 1771, apparently taking its name from *Egypt (House)* 1769, 1775. Obviously the name has been transferred from that of the country, perhaps originally on account of the relative remoteness of this area at the time. The cliff here was earlier (from the 16th century) called simply *West Cliff*, from its situation west of Cowes.

Elm Farm (south-east of Shalfleet). Recorded as *the Elme place* in 1507 and as simply *Elm* on Andrews's map of 1769. Self-explanatory, no doubt from some conspicuous elm-tree(s) growing here at an early date.

THE PLACE-NAMES OF THE ISLE OF WIGHT

Elmfield (in Ryde). A modern name, and self-explanatory.

Elmsworth Farm (near Porchfield). *Ulmesore* 1213, *Elmesore* 1220, *Elmeworthe* 1248, *Elmeshore* 1248, *Elmesworth* 1611, *Elmser (Harbour & Point)* 1769. 'The shore of the elm-tree', that is 'the shore by which elm-trees grow', from Old English *ulm*, *elm* and *ōra*. The second element was confused with Old English *worth* 'enclosed farmstead' as early as the mid-13th century, although the more historical form persisted until the 18th century. Elmsworth Saltworks are referred to as *Elmsworth Saltern* on Andrews's map of 1769, from Old English *salt-ærn* 'a building where salt was made or sold'.

Emmethill (near Kingston). Recorded as *Emmets Hill* on Andrews's map of 1769. Two early spellings, *Emedone* 1324 and *Emmotedowne* 1409, may belong here, in which case the second element has been changed from Old English *dūn* 'down' to *hill*. The first element is probably Old English *æmette* 'an ant', giving a meaning 'ant hill', or rather 'hill infested with ants' (*emmet* is in fact a dialect form of the word *ant*).

Ethel Point (in Bembridge). Part of the promontory known as Foreland, but the reason for the name is not clear.

Fairfields (2 miles south-west of Godshill). Recorded as *Fairfield* on a map of 1812, but in fact called *Bleakdown Farm* (see Bleak Down) until 1800 when it was rebuilt by the Russian merchant Michael Hoy and given its present name.

Fairlee Farm, North, & New Fairlee Farm (north-east of Newport). *Fayrlege* 1227, *le Fayrle* 1271, *Fairele* 1289, *Fayreleghe* 1517, *(New & North) Fairlee* 1769. 'The pleasant glade or woodland clearing', from Old English *fæger* and *lēah*.

Fairy Hill (near Nettlestone). So called on Wright's map of 1799, and also recorded as *Fairy Hill House* 1840. The house may have been given its whimsical name by the Rev. Henry Oglander, vicar of St Helens, who had it built in 1783.

THE DICTIONARY

Farringford Hotel (in Freshwater). This was formerly Farringford House, home of Alfred Lord Tennyson from 1852. The house dates from the mid-18th century, but the name Farringford is much older, indeed it is an ancient name dating back to early Saxon times even though the earliest recorded spellings are from the 13th century. It appears as *Feringeford* c.1250, *Feryngeford* c.1278, *Feryngford* 1293, *Faringford* 1299, and the meaning is probably 'ford of the family or followers of a man called *Fēra', from an Old English personal name with *-inga-* and *ford*. In spite of the contrasting modern spellings, it is thus identical in origin with Fringford in Oxfordshire.

Firestone Copse (near Wootton Bridge). Earlier called *Shalfleet Wood* (see Shalfleet), at least until 1750. The present name no doubt contains the word *firestone* in one of its geological senses. According to the Oxford English Dictionary, *firestone* is a popular term for iron pyrites as well as a local name for certain calcareous sandstones.

Fishbourne (near Binstead). *Fisseburne* 1267, *Fishborn Creek* 1769. 'The fish stream, the stream where fish are caught', from Old English *fisc* and *burna*. The same name is found in Sussex. The name seems to have originally referred to what is now called Wootton Creek. Nearby, on the east side of the entrance to the creek, was a place called *Fisshehous* 'the fish house', recorded from the 14th century until 1844.

Five Barrows (near Brook). Self-explanatory, referring to a group of Bronze Age burial mounds on Brook Down.

Five Barrows (near Chillerton). Like the previous name, referring to a group of Bronze Age barrows although these are no longer visible on the ground.

Five Houses (north of Calbourne). So called in 1821, a modern name, self-explanatory.

Fleetlands (near Newtown). Marked as *Flatlands* on Andrews's map of 1769, apparently earlier called *Fletplace* 1507, *Fleteplace* 1559, 'residence by the inlet or creek', from Old English *flēot* with Middle

THE PLACE-NAMES OF THE ISLE OF WIGHT

English *place*, later with *land*. At an even earlier date the surname of Geoffrey *Atteflete* 1299 ('at the creek') may have referred to the same small estuary; compare nearby Shalfleet which has a similar situation.

Ford Farm (near Whitwell). Recorded as *Ford* on Andrews's map of 1769, but earlier called *Northe forde* 1586, *Northford* 1637, 'the north ford', from Old English *north* and *ford*, to distinguish it from Southford in the same parish. At an even earlier date the local surnames *Atteford* 1271, *atte Forde* 1327, *de la Forde* 1285, 'at the ford, of the ford', may have referred to the ford that gives name to the farm.

Foreland (in Bembridge). First recorded as *East Foreland* on a map of 1591, but simply *Foreland* on Andrews's map of 1769. This is from Middle English *forelande* 'a cape, a headland, a coastal promontory', an appropriate term for what is of course the eastern extremity of the Island. The same word is found in the North Foreland and South Foreland of Kent, and in The Foreland just north of Swanage in Dorset.

Foreland Fields (in Bembridge). Like *Foreland Farm* on Andrews's map of 1769, named from Foreland; see previous name.

Forest Farm, Forest Side (west of Newport). Both named from their proximity to Parkhurst Forest.

Fort Albert (near Colwell Bay). Originally a 19th-century coastal fort (built 1856) and named after Albert, the Prince Consort; see the next name.

Fort Victoria Country Park (near Yarmouth). Named from *Fort Victoria*, a 19th-century coastal fort built (in 1854) on the site of an earlier one, and of course called after Queen Victoria; it is now almost entirely destroyed.

Freemantle Lodge (near Godshill). *Fremantel* 1285, *Fremaneshulle* 1361, *Fremantelle* 1457, *Fremantelles* 1548. A Norman-French name, literally 'the cold cloak', possibly applied figuratively to a shady wood or perhaps simply transferred from a French place. The

THE DICTIONARY

same name occurs as Freemantle in Hampshire, and is common in Northern France in the form Fromentel. It is perhaps no coincidence that the place called French Mill ('mill of the Frenchman') is not too far distant from Freemantle Lodge.

Frenchman's Hole (near Totland). A cave in the cliff, according to tradition so called because a fugitive Frenchman once hid in it and starved to death.

French Mill (1 mile east of Godshill). *molendinum de Francisco* 1316, *Frensschemulle* 1358, *Frenchmylle* 1550, *Frenche Mill* 1632. Probably 'the mill of the Frenchman', from Middle English *Frensche* and *mille* (Old English *myln*), with reference no doubt to some early tenant or owner. In the local records there is mention too of *Frensschheygh* 1358, *Frenshelond* 1364, and *Frensshefurlong* 1448, meaning 'enclosure (Old English *hæg*), cultivated land, and furlong of the Frenchman'. The stream here, which gives its name to Bathingbourne in the same parish, is called *Frenche myll brooke* in 1576.

Freshwater (medieval parish, near Totland). *Frescewatre* 1086 (Domesday Book), *Freskewatre* c.1145, *Freschewatere* 1194, *Fersshewatere* 1280, *Fresshwatre* 1322. 'Stream with fresh (i.e. not salty) water', from Old English *fersc* and *wæter*, presumably referring to one of the small upper feeders of the River Yar which rise in the south and west of the town. The River Yar itself is a tidal river, with somewhat salty water from its mouth at Yarmouth (see Saltern Wood) right up to Freshwater. The whole district to the west of the River Yar is named as *Freshwater Isle* on a map of 1611.

Freshwater Bay & Gate (near Freshwater). The former is first recorded on a map of 1550 as *Freshewater bay*. Freshwater Gate is *Freskewateresgate* c.1300, *Freshwater Gate* 1769. Middle English *gate* is here used in the sense 'gap or pass'.

Froglands Farm (in Carisbrooke). *Froglane* 1395, *Frogland* 1608, *Frogsland* 1674, *Froglands* 1781. Probably self-explanatory, 'the ground frequented by frogs', from Old English *frogga* and *land*. The place is near the stream (Lukely Brook) which gave name to Carisbrooke.

THE PLACE-NAMES OF THE ISLE OF WIGHT

Fulford (near Arreton). *Fuleford* 13th century, *Fulleford* 1395, *Fulford* 1524. 'The dirty or muddy ford', from Old English *fūl* and *ford*. This place has been identified with the Domesday Book manor of *Lamore* (1086), 'the marshy ground' from Old English *mōr* with the French definite article.

Fullholding Farm (1 mile north of Calbourne). *Fulholdynge* 1507, *Fullhalding* 1769, *Full holding* 1781. Probably 'the muddy holding or tenement', from Old English *fūl* 'foul, dirty' and Middle English *holding*. The place is quite low-lying, and near a stream.

Gallibury or Callibury Hump (on Newbarn Down south-east of Calbourne). The Bronze Age bowl barrow so called gives its name to *Gallaberry Down* 1769, *Gallybury Down* 1781. It lies high near several other tumuli and its meaning is no doubt 'the gallows hill or barrow', from Old English *galga* and *beorg*. The place-names Gawber in Yorkshire and Gowbarrow in Cumbria have the same origin. Gallibury Hump is probably referred to at a much earlier date, in a Saxon charter dated 826 describing the bounds of Calbourne, as *gemōt beorh* 'the meeting or assembly hill or barrow', from Old English *gemōt* and *beorg*.

Gallows Hill (near Arreton). Not on early record, but a gruesome name that speaks for itself. There is another Gallows Hill in Shanklin.

Garretts Farm (south-east of Newport). So called in 1862, named from its possession at some earlier date by a local family called *Garrett*; a family of this name is recorded in the St Lawrence and Gatcombe areas in 1664-5.

Garstons, Garstons Down (near Gatcombe). The latter is recorded as *Gaston Down* 1799, *Gausons Down* 1844. The names are manorial in type, indicating lands belonging at some earlier date to the local *Garston* family. Garstons Down seems to have been called *Lavendone* in 1324, probably 'down of a man called Lāfa', from an Old English personal name and *dūn*, so named as the site of a beacon. Later it was sometimes called *Gatcombe Down*, as in 1586 and 1781.

THE DICTIONARY

Gatcliff Farm (near Godshill). *Gateclyue* 1352, *Gatclyff* 1365, *Gatclefe* 1548, *Gat Clyff* 1591, *Gates Cliff* 1769. 'The steep slope or bank where goats are kept', from Old English *gāt* (genitive plural *gāta*) and *clif.*

Gatcombe (medieval parish, south of Carisbrooke). *Gatecome* 1086 (Domesday Book), *Gathecumbe* c.1220, *Gatecumb* 1223, *Gatecombe* 1261-77, *Gatecoumbe* 1316. 'The valley where goats are kept', from Old English *gāt* (genitive plural *gāta*) and *cumb*. This name is sometimes said to mean 'gateway to the valley', but this interpretation is quite incorrect; Old English *geat* 'a gate' would appear as *Yat(e)-* in an old name like this one.

Gatcombe House (in Gatcombe). This is so named on Andrews's map of 1769; like Appuldurcombe, it was once a seat of a branch of the great Worsley family.

Gatcombe Mill (near Gatcombe). Mentioned as *Watermill of Gattcombe* in 1541, *Gatcombe Mill* in 1769.

Gatehouse (near Ashey). Recorded as *Gate House* on Andrews's map of 1769, and perhaps to be associated with Nicholas *atte Gate* 1408, 'at the gate or gap', from Middle English *gate.*

Gladices (near Chale). Recorded as *Gladisses* on Andrews's map of 1769, and as *Gladices Green* in 1844; apparently earlier called *Gladhuscroft* c.1484. So named from a local family called *Gladhouse* who must have possessed land here at least as early as the 15th century. Old English *croft* means 'enclosure, small enclosed field usually attached to a house'.

Glebe Farm (near Calbourne). Self-explanatory, indicating 'farm assigned to a parish priest as part of his benefice'.

Godshill (medieval parish, 2 miles north-west of Wroxall). *Godeshul* 1142-7, *Godeshelle* c.1145, *Godeshull* 1183, *Godeshille* 1255, *Goddeshulle* 1311, *Godyshille* 1449. 'The hill associated with a heathen god, or with the Christian God', from Old English *god* and *hyll*. Although it is possible that the hill on which the 14th-century

53

church now stands was once a site of pagan worship, the first element of the name, as of Godshill in Hampshire, is quite ambiguous. However, even if the meaning is in fact 'hill of the Christian God', this may still imply a pagan site reconsecrated to Christian worship. There is certainly evidence for a Christian church here as far back as the 11th century, when it was one of the churches belonging to the Norman Abbey of Lyre. In the older records there is frequent reference to a division of the manor of Godshill known as North Godshill, the earliest being *Northgodeshulle* 1285.

Godshill Park (near Godshill). Marked as *Park* (with nearby *Park Wall*) on Andrews's map of 1769, from Middle English *park* 'an enclosed tract of land set apart for hunting'.

Golden Hill Fort (in Freshwater). The first part of this name is earlier *Gauldoune* 1299, *Gauldone* 1417, *Galdon* 1608. It probably means 'the hill or down subject to tax or rent', from Old English *gafol* and *dūn*. The later transformation to Golden is due to popular etymology. The Fort here was completed in 1867, becoming the Western District School of Gunnery from 1888 until the Second World War.

Goose Rock (near The Needles). An offshore rock called simply *The Gosse* on Speed's map of 1611, no doubt from its original resemblance to a goose.

Gore Cliff & Down (in Chale). Named from *Goore* 1591-6, *le Gore* 1608, 'the point of land or promontory', from Old English *gāra*.

Gotten Leaze (near Calbourne). *Gottone lese* 1507. A direct connection with Gotten near Chale, some 6 miles south-east of this place, is perhaps not very likely, so the first part of the name cannot be explained without earlier spellings. Leaze is from Old English *lǣs* 'pasture, meadow-land'.

Gotten Manor Farm (near Chale). *Gadetune* 1086 (Domesday Book), *Goditune* 1235, *Godeton* c.1250, *Gottone* 1409, *Gutten* 1769. 'The farmstead or estate belonging to a man called Gōda', from Old English *tūn* and an Old English personal name.

THE DICTIONARY

Grand Arch (near The Needles). An appropriately named arch of rock some 200 feet high.

Grange, Grange Chine (near Brighstone). Grange (so called on Andrews's map of 1769) is first recorded as 'the monks' grange' c.1290, later as *the Grange of Shute* 1428, *Shute* representing the present Shate Farm just to the north of Grange. In medieval times this was one of the granges of Quarr Abbey, a *grange* being 'an outlying farm belonging to a religious house where crops are stored'. The Chine is referred to as *Iacmans Chyne* in 1611, *Iackmans Chine* in 1769, so called from the *Jackman* family who held Grange in the 16th and 17th centuries.

Grange, The (1 mile north-east of Newport). Not an old name like the previous one, although all the land hereabouts belonged to Quarr Abbey in medieval times.

Great Park (1 mile west of Carisbrooke). So called on Andrews's map of 1769, with *Little Park* also marked to the south. Named from the great medieval 'park' or forest which formerly extended over a much larger area than the present Parkhurst Forest. See Newpark Farm, Park Green Farm, and Park Place Farm.

Guildford Farm (near Havenstreet). *Gylfordes* 1491, *Gylford* 1534, *Guilford* 1769. In view of the earliest spelling, probably originally a manorial name, indicating lands here once held by some family called *Gylford* who may have come from Guildford in Surrey.

Gun Hill (near Kingston). No doubt self-explanatory from some earlier gun-emplacement here.

Gunville (near Carisbrooke). First noted as *Gunvelle* or *Gunville* in 1793 for a small group of cottages around what was once called *St Austens Gate* (so named from a former chapel of St Augustine for lepers) into Parkhurst Forest. Any connection with the family of William *de Gundeville* mentioned in a Carisbrooke document of 1292 is perhaps unlikely. Mr C. D. Webster thinks it possible that Gunville may be a transferred name from Tarrant *Gunville* in Dorset (one of

THE PLACE-NAMES OF THE ISLE OF WIGHT

the daughters of Barnaby Leigh, who purchased the adjacent manor of Alvington in 1640, married a man from this Dorset place).

Gurnard, Gurnard Bay, Ledge & Pines (near Northwood). *Gornore* 1280, *Gurnore* 1333, *Gurner* 1550, *Gurnarde* 1583, *Gurnor* 1785. Probably 'the marshy or muddy shore', from Old English **gyre* 'marsh, mud' (genitive case **gyran*) and *ōra*. Gurnard Bay is so called on Andrews's map of 1769, and on the same map Gurnard Ledge is marked as *Gurnard Point*. The spelling with excrescent *-d* seems to occur from the 16th century.

Hale Manor Farm, Hale Common (1½ miles south-east of Arreton). *Atehalle* 1086 (Domesday Book), *la Hale* c.1200, *Hale* 1255, *la Haule* 1267, *Hale (Farm)* 1769. '(Place at) the nook or corner of land', from Old English *h(e)alh* (dative case *h(e)ale*). In the Domesday Book spelling, *Ate-* represents 'at the'. The manor house here is Jacobean. In the 13th century the manor was divided into *Northale* (now Hale Manor Farm) and *Southale*, this latter being further subdivided in the 14th century into Waightshale (so called from its possession by the *Wayte* family in the 15th and 16th centuries) and *Lambslease*.

Hamstead, Lower Hamstead Farm (north-west of Shalfleet). *Hamestede* 1086 (Domesday Book), *Hamested* 1160-1, *Hamstede* 1291, *Hampstede* 1327, *(East) Hampstead* 1769. 'The homestead, the site of a dwelling', from Old English *hām-stede*. The same name occurs in several other counties. There was a grange here belonging to Quarr Abbey in medieval times.

Hanover Point (near Brook). First recorded on a map of 1829 as *Hannover Point*. The first part of the name seems to be an altered and rationalized form of *Hanemouth*, the old name for nearby Brook Bay. This is *Hanemouth* 1320, *Hany mouth* 1611, 'the stony or rocky river mouth', from Old English **hānen* and *mūth*.

Harboro (on Mottistone Down north of Mottistone). *Hauedburghe* 1324, *Hawtie barrowes* 1583, *Harberows* 1596, *Harberoe Downe* 1638. 'The chief or most important hill or barrow', from Old English *hēafod* (literally 'head') and *beorg*. There is a Bronze Age barrow

56

here, and in 1324 *Hauedburghe* was the site of a defensive beacon, still shown on Speed's map of 1611.

Harbour Farm (in Bembridge). Named from its proximity to Bembridge Harbour.

Hardingshute Farm (north-west of Brading). *Hortingescet* c.1280, *Hortingsiete* c.1285, *Hortingeschit* 1306, *Hortyngshute* 1345, *Hortyngshott* 1471. 'The nook of land where whortleberries or bilberries grow', from Old English *horte* (genitive case *hortan*) and **scīete*. Alternatively the first element may be a noun **horting* meaning 'whortleberry place'.

Hardman Rock (near Mottistone). An offshore rock, but the reason for the name is not apparent.

Harts Farm (near Rookley). Named after John *Hart* who purchased a third of the farm in 1620 and held the rest on lease from the Manor of Rookley.

Haslett Farm (near Shorwell). *Haresclad* 1294, *Harslade* 1314, *Harselade* 1353, *Haselett* 1769. 'The valley frequented by hares', from Old English *hara* and *slæd*.

Hatherwood Point (near The Needles). Called *Headen Point* on Andrews's map of 1769, from nearby Headon Hill. Its present name means simply 'heather wood'.

Havenstreet (south-east of Wootton Bridge). *Hethenestrete* 1255, *la Hethenestrete* 1338, *Hethynstret* 1468, *Haven Street* 1769. This name has hitherto usually been taken to mean 'the heathen street', that is 'the street thought to have been built or used by pagans', from Old English *hǣthen* and *strǣt*, with the implication that Jutish or Saxon settlers may well have referred to an ancient track in this way. The possibility that the first element *hǣthen* has a more literal meaning 'heathy', giving a meaning 'street running through heathland', has been considered less likely. However there must be considerable doubt about both these explanations in view of the occurrence of a Richard *le Hethene* in a document relating to this area dated c.1240. This is the confirmation of a grant made by Richard *le Hethene* of a messuage and garden lying between the land of the said Richard and that of the monks of Quarr. Havenstreet may therefore after all simply mean 'the street (of houses) belonging to the man called *le Hethene*'. Of course the modern spelling, only in use since the 18th century, is the result of popular etymology, misleading the authors of the *Ward Lock Red Guide* (1970) into stating that 'the place undoubtedly was a haven at one time'!

Haylands (near Ryde). *Hillands* 1559-60, *Great, Lower & Upper Island* 1769, *Hayland's* 1771, *Haylands* 1844. Probably 'enclosed pieces of land', from Old English *hæg* and *land*.

Head Down (near Niton). *Heath downe* 1593, *Heddowne* 1608. Identical in origin and meaning with the following name.

Headon Hill & Warren (near Totland). *Heddune* c.1240, *Hetdone* 1324, *Heddenfeild* 1608, *Hedown* 1785. 'Heath hill or down', or 'hill or down where heather grows', from Old English *hǣth* 'heath, heather' and *dūn*. The Warren is referred to as *Rabbit Warren* in 1837, a *warren* being a piece of ground kept for breeding game, especially rabbits. Headon Hill was the site of a beacon in 1324.

Heasley Manor, Heasley Manor Farm (near Newchurch). *Haselie* 1086 (Domesday Book), *Haseleie* 1141-3, *Haselega* 1177, *Haselye* 1249, *Haseley* 1453. 'The wood or woodland clearing where hazels grow', from Old English *hæsel* and *lēah*. A place-name of identical origin is Haseley in Oxfordshire. The present manor house dates back mainly to the 16th century, but a 14th-century roof may be part of the original building which in medieval times was a grange belonging to Quarr Abbey.

Heathfield Farm (near Whippingham). *la Hetfeld, Hethfeld* 1341, *Heethfeld* 1438, *le Hethefeld* 1488, *Heathfield* 1769. 'The heathy open land', or 'the open land where heather grows', from Old English *hǣth* and *feld*. There are other places on the Island with this name, including one in Calbourne (*Hetfeld* 1246) and another in Freshwater (*le Hethfeld* 1299).

THE DICTIONARY

Hebberdens (1 mile east of Shalfleet). *Hoberdens place* 1517, *Heberdons* 1862. So named from a family called *Heberden*; in a 1507 rental, this tenement is said to be 'late in the possession of Richard Heberden'.

Hermitage, The (on St Catherine's Down). The present house was built in the early 19th century, but an earlier reference is to *Armytage Close* 1584, which no doubt takes its name from the medieval hermitage once situated near to where St Catherine's Oratory was erected in the early 14th century.

Hermit's Hole (north-east of Sandown). A small cavern halfway down Culver Cliff, so called on Worsley's map of 1781. Any association with an actual hermit is improbable.

High Down, Highdown Cliff (near Freshwater Bay). *Heidon, Heighdowne* 1608, *High Down* 1769. 'The high down', from Old English *hēah* and *dūn*. It is now usually called Tennyson Down.

High Hat (near St Lawrence). A high point (474 feet) on the downs, from Old English *hætt* 'a hat' often used in the sense 'hill'.

High Street (in Newport). An old street-name, first recorded as *le Higstret* in the 13th century, and meaning 'the chief or most important street', from Old English *hēah* and *strǣt*.

High Wood (near Calbourne). Self-explanatory.

Hillcross Farm (near Porchfield). Referred to as *Hillcross or Whitehouse Farm* in 1817; see Whitehouse Farm. Self-explanatory, with *cross* in the sense 'cross-roads'.

Hill Farm (1 mile north of Brading). *Heale Farm* 1560, *Hill* 1611, *Hill Farm* 1769. '(Place at) the hill', from Old English *hyll*. Mr C. D. Webster points out that this place is to be identified with the Domesday Book manor of *Witestone* (1086), later appearing (more correctly) as *Writlestun* c.1230, *Writelestone* 1235, *Wryteleston* 1299, *Writleston* 1383, a compound of Old English *tūn* 'farmstead, estate' with an Old English adjective *writol 'babbling' used substantively as the name of a 'babbling spring or stream'.

Hill Farm (near Newchurch). Recorded as *La Hulle* in 1346, and as *Hill* on Andrews's map of 1769, identical in origin with the previous name.

Hill Farm & Lodge (near Freshwater). *Hill Farm* appears on Andrews's map of 1769, earlier simply *Le Hull* 1311, '(place at) the hill', from Old English *hyll*.

Hillis Corner & Farm (near Northwood). *Hylles* 1559, *Hillis* 1608. A manorial name, indicating lands here held by the local family called *Hill(s)* who occur for instance in the Hearth Tax returns for West Cowes (John *Hill* 1664, John *Hills* 1670-1).

Hillway (near Bembridge). *Holdewaye* (probably an error for *Heldewaye*) 15th century, *Hildwaie* 1632, *Hill Way* 1823. 'The way on the slope', from Old English *helde, hielde* and *weg*.

Holden Farm (near Godshill). Recorded as *Halydon* 1535, *Houlden* 1577, *Halidon* 1620, *Holdings Fm* 1862, and previously interpreted as 'the holy hill or down' from Old English *hālig* and *dūn* (and thus often taken to be a possible pagan site, later to become the traditional site of Godshill church). However Mr C. D. Webster convincingly points out that the first part of the name represents a (now lost) place called *Haly* or *Hayle*, recorded as *Heyle* 1340, *la Heyle* 1402, *Hayle* c.1556, 'the clearing or meadow where hay is made', from Old English *hēg* and *lēah*. Thus Holden is to be interpreted as 'the down at or near *Hayle*'. A former chapel here (now a barn), first mentioned in 1305 and referred to as *Capella Halydon* in 1535, was erected by the Lisles of Appleford.

Holmewood House (near Haylands). Recorded as *Homewood* on Nichols's map of 1844. Apparently a modern name and probably self-explanatory, although the first element may represent *holm* 'holly'. There is no basis for the claim sometimes made that this is an old name containing Old English *hām*.

THE DICTIONARY

Holyrood Street (in Newport). 'The street leading to the Priory of St Cross' c.1259, *Holirodestret* 1406, *Holyrodestrete* 1469. From Old English *hālig* 'holy' and *rōd* 'cross'. 'Holy rood' is the exact equivalent of 'St Cross' in a more colloquial, native English, idiom. For the former Priory of St Cross, see Lower St Cross Farm.

Horestone Point (in Nettlestone). Recorded as *Hoo Stone Rocks* on Andrews's map of 1769. The first element represents Old English *hōh* 'a projecting piece of land, a promontory'.

Horringford (near Arreton). *Horningeforde* 1235, *Horringeford* c.1240, *Horningeford* 1255, *Horingeford* 13th century, *Horyngforde* 1333. 'The ford of the dwellers by the river fork', from Old English *horn*, *-inga-* and *ford*. The word *horn* is used of the horn-shaped tongue of land between the two streams that meet here.

Horse Ledge (near Shanklin). So called from its shape: a figurative name of a type common for coastal features.

Horseshoe Bay (off Bonchurch). So called from its shape, more pronounced on older maps.

Hoxall Cottage (near Mottistone). *Hauekeswlle* 13th century, *Haukeswulle* 1283, *Hauekeswelle* 1302, *Hoxal (Green)* 1769. 'The spring or stream of the hawk, or of a man called *Hafoc', from Old English *hafoc*, or an Old English personal name of identical form, with *wella*. The place-name Hauxwell in North Yorkshire has the same origin.

Hulverstone (near Brook). *Hunfertheston* c.1190, *Hunfredestone* c.1270, *Humerdeston* 1289, *Honfredeston* 1341, *Holverstone* 1462, *Hulverston* 1769. 'The farmstead or estate belonging to a man called Hūnfrith', from Old English *tūn* and an Old English personal name. Mr C. D. Webster points out that the Domesday Book manor of *Vlvredestune* (1086) is probably to be identified with this place (and not with Wolverton in Shorwell); this is certainly formally possible, since interchange of *-n-* and *-l-* is a common characteristic of Anglo-Norman spellings.

THE PLACE-NAMES OF THE ISLE OF WIGHT

Hunning Hall (near Brighstone). Recorded as *Honyhulle place* 1507, so originally 'honey hill' from Old English *hunig* and *hyll* like the following name.

Hunny Hill (in Newport). *Hunihille* 1228-38, *Hunyhille* 1274, *Honihill* 1289, *Honihull* c.1300, *Hony Hill* 1769. 'The hill where wild honey is to be found', from Old English *hunig* and *hyll*.

Hyde, Upper (near Shanklin). *Hyde* c.1280, *la Hyde* 1289, *atte Hyde* 1296, *la Hide* 1341, *Lower & Upper Hide* 1769. 'The hide of land', from Old English *hīd*; the form with *atte* 'at the' occurs as the surname of a person living here. A hide was an amount of land considered sufficient for the support of one free family and its dependants, usually about 120 acres. The division into a Lower and Upper Hyde seems to date back to the 18th century.

Idlecombe Down & Farm (2 miles south-west of Carisbrooke). *Idlescome* 1635, *Idlecombe* 1708. Possibly 'valley belonging to the *del Idle* or *de Lisle* family', from Old English *cumb*. Alternatively the first element may be the Old English word *īdel* used in the sense 'uncultivated'.

Itchall (1½ miles south of Godshill). *Itchilles* 1604, *Etchwell* 1769, *Itchill* 1781. From Old English **ecels*, **īecels* 'an addition, land added to an estate'.

Jeal's Lane (in Sandown). To be associated with land called *Geeles* 1632, a manorial name going back to 'the house and land of William *Juel*' recorded in c.1273. Indeed a grant of land held from John *Juell* in Nunwell occurs in a document dated c.1230.

Jobsons Farm (near Niton). Fields called *Jobson's Butt* and *Jobson's Mead* are named in a land survey of 1771, all indicating lands held by a local family called *Jobson* mentioned in 17th-century records. The dialect word *butt* means 'short strip of land'.

Keats Green (in Shanklin). Named to commemorate the poet John Keats who stayed in Shanklin in 1819 and here completed the first book of his poem *Lamia* and part of his play *Otho the Great*.

THE DICTIONARY

Kennerley Farm (near Godshill). *Kenewardle* 1202, *Kynewardle* 1285, *Kenwarle* 1327, *Kennerley* 1578, *Great & Little Kinnerly* 1769. 'Woodland clearing belonging to a man called Cyneweard', from Old English *lēah* and an Old English personal name. The place-name Kennerleigh in Devon is identical in origin. Kennerley Farm was formerly *Little Kennerley*.

Kern Farm (near Alverstone). *Lacherne* 1086 (Domesday Book), *Querna* 13th century, *la Curne* 1203, *Kurne* 1279, *Kern* c.1440. From Old English *cweorn, cwyrn* 'a quern, a mill', with the French definite article in the Domesday and 1203 forms.

Kingates (near Niton). *Kingates* 1635, *Kingetts* 1812, *Kingsgate* 1844. A manorial name, indicating lands here held by a local family called *Kyngot* mentioned in 14th-century documents.

King's Manor (near Freshwater). Called *Freshwater Farm* on Andrews's map of 1769, and known by this name until earlier this century. The present name recalls the medieval manor of 'King's Freshwater': this was at one time a royal manor, granted by Edward I in 1301 for the maintenance of his daughter Mary at the Benedictine Abbey of Amesbury in Wiltshire.

King's Oak (in Bembridge). Planted in 1902 to commemorate the Coronation of King Edward VII.

King's Quay (near Whippingham). *Kings Haven* 1693, *Kings Key* 1769. Said to have been so named from a fanciful but colourful tradition that King John retired here to sulk after signing Magna Carta, leading, according to the 13th-century chronicler Roger of Wendover, 'a solitarie lyfe among reivers (i.e. pirates) and fishermen' (*Red Guide*). There was formerly a settlement and manor here (on the west side of the creek) called *Shoflet*, recorded in the Domesday Book of 1086 as *Soflet*, later as *Shoesfleth* c.1248, *Schoufflet* 14th century, *Showflyt* 1550. This is from Old English *flēot* 'a creek or estuary' with a first element Old English *scōh* 'a shoe', probably with reference to 'a shoe-shaped promontory or spit of land'.

THE PLACE-NAMES OF THE ISLE OF WIGHT

Kingston (medieval parish, 2 miles south-east of Shorwell). *Chingestune* 1086 (Domesday Book), *Kyngeston* c.1240, *Kyngestone* 1250, *Kingestone* 1255, *Kingston* 1375. 'The king's manor or estate, the royal manor', from Old English *cyning* and *tūn*. There are examples of this name in several English counties, including Hampshire and Dorset.

Kingston Farm (in Whippingham). *Kingston* on Andrews's map of 1769, but called *Little Kingston* in 1659. This is a manorial name, so called from its former possession by the *Kingston* family of Kingston (see previous name).

Kitbridge Farm (near Newport). Recorded as *Cutebrigge* c.1220, 1270, and as *Ketbridge (Barn)* on Andrews's map of 1769. 'The bridge frequented by kites', from Old English *cȳta, cēta* and *brycg*. There must have been an early bridge over the small stream here.

Kite Hill (near Fishbourne). *Kete* c.1450, *Kytehylle* 1491, *Kite Hill* 1769. If the earliest spelling is correct, first element probably Old English *cyte, cete* 'a cottage' rather than Old English *cȳta, cēta* 'a kite', with Old English *hyll*.

Knighton Farm (near Newchurch). *Chenistone* 1086 (Domesday Book), *Cnihtaton* 1193-1217, *Knyttetone* 1255, *Knyghteton* 1316, *Knightone* 1327. 'The farmstead or estate of the young thanes or retainers', from Old English *cniht* (genitive plural *cnihta*) and *tūn*. There are examples of this name in several English counties, including Dorset and Wiltshire.

Knight's Farm (east of Newport). This place and nearby Knight's Cross are named from a local family called *Knight* recorded elsewhere in the area at an early date: a family of this name were tenants of Quarr Abbey at *Claybrooke* (now Binfield) in the 15th century, and a holding called *Knyghtescroft* in 1385 may have been at North Fairlee.

Knowles (in Bembridge). Called *Knowles Fm* on Albin's map of 1823. Identical in origin with the following name.

64

THE DICTIONARY

Knowles Farm (near Niton). *Knolles* 1450, *Knowles* 1584, *Knoles* 1608. Probably a manorial name, indicating land here held by a local family called *Knoll*, of whom Richard *Knol*, bailiff of Niton, is mentioned as early as 1270. The origin of this surname is Old English *cnoll* 'a hillock', a word also occurring as a place-name in this vicinity in the reference *viam que duxit ad Cnollam* ('the road which leads to Cnoll') in a document dating from the early 13th century.

Lake (in Sandown). Appearing as *Lake* on Andrews's map of 1769, but first named in a document of c.1225 which records a grant of land including '½ part of *Lake*', and probably also to be associated with William *atte Lake* 1280. The origin is Old English *lacu* 'a stream', here referring to a small tributary of the River Yar. There is another place called Lake, with the same origin, in Gatcombe. In medieval times the area now called Lake was more often known as *Suth Sandham* 1241, *Southsandham* 1316; see Sandown.

Lambsleaze (near Locksgreen). First recorded as *Lambs Leaze* on Andrews's map of 1769, 'pasture for lambs', from Old English *lamb* and *lǣs*.

Landguard Manor (near Shanklin). *Langrad* 1255, *Langrede* 1279, *Langerud* 14th century, *Langarde* 1499, *Great & Little Languard* 1769. 'The long reed-bed', from Old English *lang* and *hrēod*.

Landslip, The (near Bonchurch). This beautiful area of tangled trees and undergrowth beneath the cliffs takes its name from the heavy falls of rock and earth here in the early 19th century.

Lane End (in Bembridge). First recorded in 1856, earlier called *Brookend* on Taylor's map of 1759. Both names are self-explanatory.

Langbridge (near Newchurch). *Langhebrigge* 1228, *Langbrigg* c.1290, *Langebrigge*, *Longebrugge* 13th century, *Langbridge* 1781. 'The long bridge', from Old English *lang* and *brycg*. The road from Newchurch crosses the River Yar here. There is another Langbridge of identical origin, also dating back to the 13th century, in Calbourne.

THE PLACE-NAMES OF THE ISLE OF WIGHT

Lea Farm (1 mile west of Sandown). *Alalei* 1086 (Domesday Book), *La Lee* 1241, *Leygh* 1332. Identical in origin with the next name. The Domesday spelling (which probably belongs here) represents a 'Frenchified' *à la Lei* for an original Old English *æt thǣm lēa* '(place) at the wood or clearing'.

Leechmore Farm (near Godshill). Named from *Leechmore Pond*, called *Lashmere* or *Lechmere Pond* in 1856, 'the pool where leeches are to be found', from Old English *lǣce* and *mere* (with the addition of 'explanatory' *pond*).

Lee Copse & Lee Farm (near Thorley). Both named from *la Lye* 1279, *la Leyghe* 1299, *La Lee* 1344, *Leighe* 1608. 'The wood or woodland clearing', from Old English *lēah*, with the French definite article in the early forms.

Lessland Farm (near Godshill). *Liscelande, Litesland* 1086 (Domesday Book), *Lucelond* c.1235, *Lecceland* 1291, *Lescelond* 1305. 'Enclosed piece of cultivated land', or 'piece of cultivated land with an enclosure', from Old English **lycce* and *land*.

Limerstone, Limerstone Down (near Brighstone). *Lemerestune* 1252, *Lemerstone* 1265, *Lumerestune* 1273, *Lymerstone* 1291, *Lemerstone (Down)* 1769. 'The farmstead or estate belonging to a man called Lēofmǣr or Lēodmǣr', from Old English *tūn* and an Old English personal name.

Linstone Chine (near Totland). Recorded as *Levenchin* 1608, apparently 'chine of a man called Lēofwine' from Old English *cinu* and an Old English personal name. A place recorded as *Leynestone* 1271, *Lenestone* 1280, 'Lēofwine's farmstead or estate', from Old English *tūn* and the same personal name, was probably near here, giving the modern form Linstone.

Little London (in Newport). So called on Andrews's map of 1769, named no doubt from the former commercial activity of the area near the quay.

THE DICTIONARY

Little Stairs Point (near Shanklin). No doubt self-explanatory. Its first mention as *Litterstairs* on Taylor's map of 1759 must be an error; it is correctly *Little Stairs* on Andrews's map of 1769.

Littletown (near Wootton Bridge). Recorded as *Little Town* on Andrews's map of 1769, self-explanatory.

Locksgreen (1 mile east of Newtown). To be associated with *Lokkesland* 1387, *Lockesplace* 1507, *(Little) Locks* 1769, all named from a local family called *Lokke* who must have possessed land here at least as early as the 14th century.

Lodge Farm (in Calbourne). Earlier called *Calbourn Lodge* 1793, *Frogwell or Calbourne Lodge* 1813, *Calbourne Lodge* 1862.

London Farm (1 mile north-east of Shalfleet). Named as *London* in 1508 and 1664 and on Andrews's map of 1769. Transferred names of this kind are often given ironically to rather remote or isolated farms or pieces of land, but compare Little London in Newport for a quite different significance.

Long Copse (near Gatcombe). Self-explanatory.

Longdown (near Merstone). *Langedune* 1299, *Langedone* 1341, *Langedon* 1349, *Longdown* 1769. 'The long hill or down', from Old English *lang* and *dūn*.

Longlands (near Brading). *le Langelonde* 15th century, *Langland* 1769. 'The long piece of cultivated land', from Old English *lang* and *land*.

Long Ledge (in Bembridge). An offshore ledge of rock, called *Bembridge Ledge* on Worsley's map of 1781.

Longstone, The (in Mottistone). Called *Long Stone* on Andrews's map of 1769. This huge quadrangular pillar of iron sandstone (once part of a Neolithic long barrow) standing on the hill above the village of Mottistone must have been 'the stone of the speaker or speakers' which gave its name to the place. See Mottistone.

THE PLACE-NAMES OF THE ISLE OF WIGHT

Lord Holmes's Cellar & Parlour (near The Needles). Caves in the cliff, according to tradition so called because the gallant Admiral Sir Robert Holmes, Governor or Captain of the Island from 1667 to 1692, kept his wine in the former and entertained his guests in the latter!

Loverston Farm (near Chillerton). *Levegarestun* 1086 (Domesday Book), *Leuestone* 1299, *Loverston* c.1286, *Louerstone* 1340, *Laviston* 1769. 'The farmstead or estate belonging to a man called Lēofgār', from Old English *tūn* and an Old English personal name.

Lower Rill (near Chillerton), see under Rill.

Lower St Cross Farm (north of Newport). Named from the former priory of St Cross, a cell of the Benedictine abbey of Tiron (Eure-et-Loir, France), founded in 1120 and well recorded in medieval documents from the 12th to 15th century: *Sancte Crucis* c.1140, *Sancta Cruce* 1255, *Seyntecros* 1418, *Saynte Crosse* 1559, that is 'the holy cross' from Middle English *seint* 'holy' and *cros*. Also named from the priory is Saint Cross Mill (on Lukely Brook), earlier *Seintcrosse mylle* 1466.

Lower Yard (near Godshill), see Yard.

Lowtherville (in Ventnor). A modern name for an area of the town developed in the late 19th century, also sometimes known as Upper Ventnor. Originally called simply *Lowther* from the surname of the principal landowner, Captain Francis *Lowther*.

Luccombe Bay & Chine (near Shanklin). See next name. Luccombe Chine is so called on Worsley's map of 1781 (from Old English *cinu* 'a ravine'), and *Luccumb Chine Head* is marked on Andrews's map of 1769. In an account dated 1790 and on a map of 1851 it has the alternative name *Bowl Hoop*, 'the bowl-shaped bay', from Old English *bolla* and *hōp*.

Luccombe Village (near Shanklin). *Lovecumbe* 1086 (Domesday Book), *Louecomba* 1141-3, *Luvecumbe* 1258, *Lovecombe* 1291, *Luckome* 1611, *Luccumb* 1769. Probably 'the valley belonging to a man called Lufa', from Old English *cumb* and an Old English personal name. However it is possible that the first element is the

THE DICTIONARY

word *lufu* 'love', in which case the name would be an allusion to a secluded spot considered suitable for courtship and love-making! The same name occurs in Somerset. There was a grange here belonging to Quarr Abbey in medieval times.

Lucketts (near Bouldnor). Appearing as *Loketts* in 1560 and as *Luckits* on Andrews's map of 1769, but with its present spelling in a land survey of 1771, no doubt a manorial name indicating land here held at some date by a local family called *Lockett* or *Luckett*.

Ludham Cottage (near Whippingham). So called on the Ordnance Survey map of 1862, origin uncertain.

Lugley Street (in Newport). *Leggellestrete* c.1275, *Lugalaystret* 13th century. Named from the family of William *Logele* or *Lugelay*, mentioned in records from c.1260 as provost or reeve of Newport.

Lukely Brook (the stream flowing through Carisbrooke). 'stream of *Lokeleie*' c.1191, *Lukelie* c.1230, *Loclie* c.1253, 'stream called *Luckleye*' 14th century, *Lukkeley* 1413. The second element is Old English *lēah* 'woodland clearing or meadow', the first a postulated Old English word **luca* or **lūce* meaning something like 'a barrier in a stream to form a pool, a mill-dam'. It is perhaps no coincidence that one Alurich *le Lokere* is mentioned c.1200-30 as having lands in this vicinity: his surname would seem to mean 'the one in charge of the river-barrier or dam'. Mr C. D. Webster points out that in 1627 there were no fewer than 7 water mills on Lukely Brook, in the area immediately west of Newport.

Luton Farm (near Northwood). *Levintun(e)* 1086 (Domesday Book), *Leuitona* mid-12th century, *Leuetone* 1337, *Luton* 1769. Probably 'the farmstead or estate belonging to a man called Lēofa', from an Old English personal name (genitive case *Lēofan*) and Old English *tūn*.

Lynch (in Calbourne). *Linch* 1608, from Old English *hlinc* 'a ridge, a bank'.

Lynn Farm (2 miles east of Newport). *le Lyn* 1487, *Lyn* 1524, *Lyne*, *Lynehedde* 1534, *Lynn* 1608. 'The noisy brook or torrent', from Old

THE PLACE-NAMES OF THE ISLE OF WIGHT

English *hlynn*, originally with reference to the stream known as Deadman's Brook. The form *Lynehedde* contains Old English *hēafod* 'river spring or source'.

Main Bench (near The Needles). So called on Andrews's map of 1769. The word *bench* is here used in a topographical sense 'flat-topped cliff'.

Mall, The (in Brading). To be associated with a field called *Mall Ground* in 1823, and named from the word *mall* 'a sheltered walk serving as a promenade'. Mr C. D. Webster notes another example of the same name, The Mall, in Newport, a raised footpath running from Newport to Carisbrooke parallel to the main Carisbrooke road. The word *mall* originally referred to the game called *mall* or *pall-mall* in which a ball was struck by a mallet through an iron ring, played in London in the 17th century (hence the London street-names The Mall and Pall Mall which were at one time alleys where this game was played).

Mark's Corner (1 mile south-west of Northwood). Named after one *Mark* Harvey who had land here in the 17th century.

Marshgreen Farm (in Brighstone). *Marsh Green* on Andrews's map of 1769. Like *Mersh place* 1507, named from *la Merse* 1248, *le Mersche* 1383, 'the marshy ground', from Old English *mersc*.

Marsh House (near Brading). So named on Andrews's map of 1769, but built before 1620. It lies within part of *North Marsh* (also marked on Andrews's map) which was drained from Brading Harbour in 1562. Probably to be associated with *Mersshe* 1431, from Old English *mersc* as in the previous name.

Marvel Farm (south of Newport). *Mirifeld* 1235, *Meriefeld* 1255, *Murifelde* 1311, *Marvell* 1608. 'The pleasant open country', or 'the open country where merry-making takes place', from Old English *myrge* and *feld*. It will be noted that the modern spelling, representing a dialect pronunciation of the original name, first appears in the 17th century.

THE DICTIONARY

Medham House (in Northwood). Recorded as *Medham* 1626, *Midham* 1781, and possibly to be associated with William *de Medeme* 1299. So called from the old name of the River Medina, near to which it is situated.

Medina, River. *Medine* c.1200, *Medeme* 13th century, *Medme* 1279, *Medome* 1299, *Medene* 1769. 'The middle one', i.e. 'the river in the middle of the Island', from Old English *medume, meodume* 'middle'. The River Meden in Nottinghamshire has the same origin (being the middle one of three rivers). The River Medina rises at the foot of St Catherine's Down in the south of the Island, thence traversing it to flow northward into the Solent at Cowes. The River also gave name to the two Hundreds of East and West Medine into which the Island was divided, these dating back to the 12th century.

Merrie Gardens (near Shanklin). Called *Cherry Gardens* on Andrews's map of 1769, but *Merry Gardens* on Wright's plan of 1799. The word *merry* is in fact local dialect for 'the common black or wild cherry'.

Mersley Down, Mersley Farms (1 mile north of Newchurch). *Maddokesley* c.1250, *Madekeslie* c.1270, *Markesley* 16th century, *Messly* 1769. 'The woodland clearing or meadow belonging to a man (or family) called Madoc(k)', from Old English *lēah* with an originally Welsh personal name. Mersley Down, named from the settlement, appears as *Messly Down* on Andrews's map of 1769.

Merston Manor, Merstone (near Arreton). *Messetone, Merestone* 1086 (Domesday Book), *Merston* c.1200, *Merstone* 1271, *Mershton* 1349. 'The farmstead by the marsh', or 'the farmstead on marshy ground', from Old English *mersc* and *tūn*. Merston in Sussex has the same origin. The manor house itself dates back to 1615.

Middleton (in Freshwater). *Medeltone* 1246, *Mideltune* 1283, *Middeltone* 1327, *Myddeltone* 15th century. 'The middle farmstead or estate', from Old English *middel* and *tūn*. It is named from its situation between Easton and Weston.

THE PLACE-NAMES OF THE ISLE OF WIGHT

Mill Farm (at Bembridge). Named from Bembridge Windmill, a stone tower mill, and the last remaining windmill on the Island, built about 1700.

Monks Bay (off Bonchurch). According to one tradition so called because the monks of the Norman Abbey of Lyre habitually landed here when coming over to visit their many estates on the Island in medieval times. However it is perhaps more likely that the name commemorates the fact that the living of Bonchurch was once in the gift of the Abbey of Christchurch Twynham, or that the Abbey of Quarr had a grange at nearby Luccombe in medieval times and also had lands on St Boniface Down (confirmed in a deed from the early 13th century).

Monktonmead Brook (south of Ryde). Named from *Monken Meade* 1544, 'the meadow of the monks', from Old English *munuc* (with later dialect plural *-en*) and *mǣd*; earlier referred to as 'the meadow of *Prestitun* (i.e. Preston)' 1215, at which date it belonged to the monks of Quarr Abbey. The brook was earlier called *Smalbroke*; see Smallbrook Farm.

Moor Farm (near Godshill). *Lamore* 1086 (Domesday Book), *la More* 13th century, *Attemore* 1288, *More* c.1450, *Moore* 1769. 'The marshy ground', from Old English *mōr*, with the French definite article in the early spellings. The form *Attemore* occurs as a surname and means '(living) at the marshy ground'.

Moortown (in Brighstone). '(township of) *More*' 1248, *Mortone* 1320, *Mourton* 1383. Originally 'the marshy ground' from Old English *mōr*, later with the addition of *tūn* 'farmstead, hamlet'.

Morton, Morton Manor (near Brading). *la Mortone* 1267, *Morton* 1311, *Moureton* 1317, *la Mourtone* 15th century. 'The farmstead or estate in marshy ground', from Old English *mōr* and *tūn*. It is spelt *Martin* on 18th- and 19th-century maps, reflecting the local pronunciation.

Mottistone (medieval parish, near Brook). *Modrestan* 1086 (Domesday Book), *Motestan* 1176, *Moterestone* 1291, *Mottistone* 1374. 'The stone of the speaker or speakers at a meeting', from Old

THE DICTIONARY

English *mōtere* and *stān*. This name, originally applied by the Jutes or Saxons to the large menhir (now called The Longstone) standing on the hill above the village, must have been transferred to the settlement here long before its appearance in Domesday Book. The stone itself, already 3000 years old when given its name by the Jutes or Saxons, clearly became an important meeting-place for certain judicial or official procedures during the Anglo-Saxon period.

Mottistone Down (near Mottistone). First recorded as *Motson Downe* in 1638, then as *Mottestone Down* in 1769.

Mount Bay (off St Lawrence). Named from an old local family called *le Mount* who also gave name to *Mount's Farm* 1620.

Mount Misery (1 mile south of Whippingham). A derogatory name for land considered unproductive or difficult to cultivate. A name of similar meaning, *Small Gains*, is marked near here on Andrews's map of 1769. Fortunately its opposite, the complimentary name Mount Pleasant, is much more frequent: there are examples in Carisbrooke, Newchurch and Shalfleet.

Mudless Copse (east of Calbourne). Origin uncertain, although it was called *Great Wood* in 1862.

Nansen Hill (near Bonchurch). Part of the Down overlooking the Landslip presented to the nation in 1934 by Mr Howard Whitehouse to commemorate the famous Norwegian explorer, Fridtjof *Nansen* (1861-1930).

Needles, The. The three famous chalk stacks off the western point of the Island are recorded as *Nedlen* 1333, *les Nedeles* 1409, *The Nedles* 1583, *The Nedells* 1600. The name is self-explanatory, from Old English *nǣdl*, referring to their pointed shape. A fourth rock, known as *Lot's Wife*, with a particularly slender outline about 120 feet high, collapsed in 1764. The 14th-century spelling *Nedlen* represents an old dialect plural form, with *-en* instead of *-es*. The Needles give their name to Needles Down and to the Needles Lighthouse, built in 1858.

THE PLACE-NAMES OF THE ISLE OF WIGHT

Neptunes Caves (near The Needles). Deep caves in the cliffs, appropriately enough named from the Roman god of the sea.

Nettlecombe (near Whitwell). *Netelcumba* c.1200, *Netelcumbe* 1253, *Ntelcumbe* (sic) 1271, *Netelcombe* 1351, *Netylcombe* 1417. 'The valley where nettles grow', from Old English *netele* and *cumb*. There are places with the same name in Dorset and Somerset.

Nettlestone (north of St Helens). *Hoteleston(e)* (sic) 1086 (Domesday Book), *Nutelastone* 1248, *Nottlestone* 1267, *Notelestone* 1269, *Netleston* 1352. 'The farmstead in or near the nut-tree pasture or nut-tree wood', from Old English *hnutu*, $l\bar{æ}s$ or $l\bar{e}ah$ (genitive case $l\bar{e}as$), and $t\bar{u}n$. By the 14th century the original meaning of the name was probably no longer understood, hence the change to the modern form through association of the first part of the name with the word *nettle*.

Nettlestone Point (near Nettlestone). Called *Nettles Heath Point* on Avery's map of 1720, which is to be associated with *Nettles Hythe* on Speed's map of 1611. From Old English $h\bar{y}th$ 'a harbour, a landing-place', *Nettles* representing a shortened form of Nettlestone.

Newbarn Down, Newbarn Farm (near Calbourne). So called on Worsley's map of 1781, self-explanatory. Mr C. D. Webster notes that the barn was moved from Swainston House in 1629 when the farm was created out of the western part of Swainston demesne.

New Barn Farm, Newbarn Down (near Shorwell). Self-explanatory, see previous name.

Newbridge (south of Shalfleet). *Newbryge* 1378. 'The new bridge', from Old English $n\bar{\imath}we$ and *brycg*. The road to Calbourne crosses the stream called Caul Bourne here.

Newchurch (medieval parish, 2 miles west of Sandown). *Niechirche* c.1150, *Niucherche* 1171, *Newecherche* 1228, *Neuchirche* 1255, *Nywechurche* 1279. 'The new church', from Old English $n\bar{\imath}we$ and *cirice*. The church was in fact 'new' in the 11th century, for it was founded in 1087 (or perhaps even earlier, for it is named as one of the

THE DICTIONARY

churches belonging to the Norman Abbey of Lyre in 1070). The same name is found in Kent.

New Close House (near Carisbrooke). *Newclose* 1703. Self-explanatory, 'the new enclosure'.

New Farm (in Brading). Recorded thus in 1862, though built c.1810. Self-explanatory.

Newnham Farm (near Binstead). *Nyweham* c.1150, *Neweham* 1255, *Nywenham* 1279, *Newenham* 1284, *Ninham* 1759. 'The new homestead or enclosure', from Old English *nīwe* (dative case *nīwan*) and *hām* or *hamm*. The 18th-century spelling *Ninham* represents the local pronunciation of the name still current. This farm is on the site of the home grange of Quarr Abbey.

Newpark Farm (west of Carisbrooke). *Novo Parco* 1334, *New Park* 1769. Self-explanatory, with the early form in Latin. Named from its having been part of the great medieval 'park' or forest which formerly extended over a much larger area than the present Parkhurst Forest. See Great Park, Park Green Farm and Park Place Farm.

Newport (ancient borough and the Island's capital). *Novo Burgo* 1189-1204, *Neweport* 1202, *Neuport* 1227, *Niweport* 1279, *Newporte* 1307. 'The new harbour or market town', from Old English *nīwe* and *port*. The earliest spelling (the ablative case of Latin *novus burgus*) is common in medieval sources. The same name is found in Devon and other English counties. Newport received its first borough charter from Richard de Redvers, 4th Earl of Devon, between 1188 and 1193.

Newtown (north of Shalfleet). *Niwetune* 1189-1204, *nouum burgum de Francheuile* 1254, *Newtone* 1255, *Frauncheuile* 1257, *la Nywetone* 1339, *Newtowne alias Frauncheuyle* 1512. 'The new town or borough', from Old English *nīwe* and *tūn*, but from early times alternatively called *Francheville*, that is 'the free town', from Old French *franche* and *ville*. This name seems to have been used alongside Newtown up to the 16th century, since which time only the present name has been in use. The town received its charter from the Bishop of Winchester in 1256. The name 'free town' no doubt implies some fiscal autonomy in the levying of taxes, with freedom from interference and control by royal or feudal agents, as well as freedom from tolls on traded goods.

Newtown Bay, Newtown River. Both named from Newtown, the Bay being so called (*New Town Bay*) on Andrews's map of 1769. The estuary of Newtown River was known as *Newtowne haven* 1583, *Newton haven* 1611, from Old English *hæfen* 'a harbour, a landing-place'; see also Western Haven. These names are a reminder that Newtown was once a sizeable port before the river and harbour silted up.

Ningwood, Ningwood Manor Farm, Ningwood Common (near Shalfleet). *Lenimcode* (sic) 1086 (Domesday Book), *Ningewode* 1189-1204, *Nynngewode* c.1210, *Ningwode* 1250-60, *Nyngewode* 1279. 'The wood that has been partly enclosed or taken into cultivation', from Old English **niming* 'land enclosed or taken into cultivation' and *wudu*. In the Domesday spelling *Le-* represents the French definite article. *Ningwood Common* and *Ningwood Green* are marked on Andrews's map of 1769.

Ninham (near Shanklin). According to Mr C. D. Webster a manorial name first recorded as *Newnhams* 1566 (later spellings are *Newnham* 1619, *Ninham* 1627), so called from its possession by William *Newnham* of Newport who apparently took his name from a lost settlement of *Newnham* at Chale (this having the same origin as Newnham in Binstead).

Niton (medieval parish, 2 miles west of St Lawrence). *Neeton* 1086 (Domesday Book), *Neuton* 1155-8, *Nitona* 1189-1204, *Niweton* 1193-1217, *Nyton* 1305. 'The new farmstead or settlement', from Old English *nīwe*, **nīge* and *tūn*. The development to *Ni-* from an old dialect form **nīge* is found also in the place-names of South-East England, Nyton in West Sussex having the same origin. Niton was at one time known locally as 'Crab Niton' from the abundance of crabs caught off the coast here.

Nodes Farm (in Northwood). Recorded thus in 1700 and to be associated with *Nodefield* 1625. There was a beacon site here in early

THE DICTIONARY

times, and the form *Node* is from Middle English *atten ode* '(place) at the beacon', from Old English *ād* 'beacon', the initial *N-* being a remnant of the old definite article.

Node's Point (near St Helens). Earlier called *St. Elaines Poynt* 1539, *St. Helyns Point* 1545, from its proximity to St Helens. The present name contains the old word *ād* 'beacon' as in the previous name; this was also the site of a defensive beacon at least as early as the 14th century.

Nodewell Farm & The Nodes (near Freshwater Bay). No doubt to be associated with Randolph *del Ode* c.1240, Henry *de la Ode* c.1250, Adam *atten Ode* 1311 (all mentioned in connection with Freshwater) and *Nodeclose* 1630 (in Freshwater). All these names contain Old English *ād* 'beacon' as in the previous two names. They suggest that there must have been a defensive beacon on the Down here in very early times, and indeed the Nodes Beacon (marked *Beacon* on Andrews's map of 1769) seems to have been on or near the spot now occupied by the monument to Alfred Lord Tennyson.

Noke Farm (near Parkhurst). Recorded as *Noke* in 1547 and on Andrews's map of 1769. From Middle English *atten oke* '(place) at the oak-tree', the initial *N-* being a remnant of the old definite article.

No Man's Land Fort (off Ryde). This fort is on an artificial island in Spithead Channel. The name *No Man's Land* was often given to a particularly remote or desolate spot.

Norris Castle (in East Cowes). Built in 1799, and taking its name from an estate called *Norys* 1519, *Norres* 1559, *Norris* 1611. This is a manorial name, indicating lands held here in the 14th century by a family called *(le) Noreys* who also owned Atherfield Farm.

North Court (in Shorwell). First recorded as *North Court* in 1608, but earlier called *Northsorewelle* 1285, *Northschorewelle* 1302, *Northeshorewelle* 1541, that is 'the north manor of Shorwell'; compare West Court which was originally 'the south manor of Shorwell'. Both manors are recorded in the Domesday Book of 1086 as *Sorewelle*. The word *court* is used here in the sense 'manor house';

THE PLACE-NAMES OF THE ISLE OF WIGHT

North Court, stone-built in the early 17th century, is the largest in the Island.

North Grounds (near Chale Green). Recorded thus in 1613 and 1669. Self-explanatory, this place being in the north of Chale parish.

Northwood (medieval parish, near Cowes). *Nortwuda* 1181-5, *Northwwde* early 13th century, *Northwode* 1248, *Northewode* 1250-60, *Northwoode* 1535. 'The northern wood', from Old English *north* and *wudu*, so called from its situation north of the great medieval forest of Parkhurst.

Northwood House (in West Cowes). Built in the early 19th century on the site of a former house called *Belle Vue*. Named from nearby Northwood.

Norton, Norton Green (near Freshwater). *Northone* 1248, *Nortone* 1271, *Norton* 1608. 'The northern farmstead or estate', from Old English *north* and *tūn*. It is named from its situation to the north of Freshwater. Norton Green is called *More Green* on some 18th-century maps, so named from a lost place called *le More* 1299, 'the moor or marshy ground', from Old English *mōr*.

Nunneys Wood (near Shalfleet). *Noneleas Wood* 1544, *Munleaze Wood* (sic) 1862. Possibly 'the pasture or meadow-land of the nuns', from Old English *nunne* and *lǣs*. Alternatively the name may be manorial in type, indicating lands formerly held here by a family called *Nunley* or the like.

Nunwell, Nunwell Farm (near Brading). *Nonoelle* 1086 (Domesday Book), *Nunewell* c.1150, *Nonnawelle* 1193-1217, *Nunnewelle* c.1226, *Nunwell* 1541. Either 'the spring or stream of a man called Nunna', from Old English *wella* and an Old English personal name, or 'the spring or stream of the nuns' if the first element is rather Old English *nunne* 'nun'. The stream referred to (also called *Nunnebroc* 'Nunna's brook' in the 13th century) is that rising near Nunwell Farm. The farm itself is recorded on Worsley's map of 1781. Nunwell manor is the ancient seat of the famous Island family called *Oglander*, who seem to have held it in direct descent from the time of Henry I until 1874.

THE DICTIONARY

Oakfield (in Ryde). Self-explanatory. The same name occurs in Cowes and Whippingham.

Oak Hill (in Seaview). A self-explanatory modern name.

Old Castle Point (in East Cowes). So called on Andrews's map of 1769, named from one of the forts built by Henry VIII to defend the Island against attack from the French and Spanish. The fort in question, once called *the Est Cow* from its situation on the east side of the Medina estuary (see Cowes), was in ruins by the 17th century and has since disappeared.

Old Park (near St Lawrence). So named on Andrews's map of 1769. The property so called takes its name from the 'park' which once extended from Bonchurch to Niton, recorded as *S. Laurence park* on Speed's map of 1611, this no doubt representing a medieval *park* in the sense 'enclosed tract of ground set apart for the breeding and hunting of wild animals'.

Orchard Cove (off St Lawrence). Sometimes called *Orchard's Bay* when first recorded in the early 1900s. Named from a local family called *Orchard* who also held The Orchard in Niton.

Orchard, The (in Niton). Originally *Orchards*, taking its name from a family known in Niton since 1379.

Osborne, Osborne House, Osborne Bay (near East Cowes). *Austeburn* 1316, *Austebourne* 1327, *Austerborn* 1339, *Auseborne* 1514, *Osborne* 1559. Probably 'the stream at the sheepfold', from Old English *eowestre* and *burna*. Thus the humble origins of this place, destined later to be the site of Queen Victoria's grand Italianate palace, Osborne House, completed in 1848! The area behind Osborne bay was formerly called *the Medehole* 1514, *Meadehole* 1550, *Meade hole* 1600, 'the meadow hollow or valley', from Old English *mǣd* and *hol*.

Packsfield (near Wootton Bridge). *Packesfeude* 13th century, *Pakesfeld* 1488, *Packsfield* 1862. 'Open land belonging to a man called *Pæcc', from Old English *feld* and an Old English personal name.

Padmore (in Whippingham). *Paddemore* c.1247, *Paddemour* 1342, *Padmore* 1442. 'The marshy ground frequented by toads', from Old English *padde* and *mōr*.

Pagham Farm (near Rookley). *Merstone* 1299, *Merstone Pageham* 14th century, *Southmerschton* 1352, *Pagham* 1480. This was originally the southern part of the manor of Merston, called *Merstone Pageham* because it was held by the *de Pageham* family (no doubt taking their name from Pagham in Sussex) as early as 1299. Since the 15th century the manorial affix has been used on its own.

Pallance Farm, Pallancegate (near Northwood). *Pallanthill* 1608, *Pallance* 1664, *Greate Pallants* 1708, *Pallanst, Pallans Gate* 1781. A manorial name, indicating lands here held by the family of Nicholas *de La Palente* (here in 1235). The family originated from The Pallant in Chichester, Sussex, a name derived from Old English *palant* 'a district in which the Archbishop of Canterbury had special palatine rights'. The 'gate' at Pallancegate was no doubt one into Parkhurst Forest.

Palmer's Brook (near Whippingham). So called on Andrews's map of 1769, named from *Palmers* 1521, a manorial name indicating lands here formerly held by the local *Palmer* family, and no doubt to be identified with 'the land of John *Palmer*, late John Coterel, in *Wooditon* (= Wootton)' 1352.

Pan, Great Pan Farm (in Newport). *Lepene* 1086 (Domesday Book), *Penna* 1204, *la Penne* 1217, *Panne* c.1274, *Pan* 1611, *Pann* 1769. '(Place at) the pen or fold for animals', from Old English *penn*. The development from *Pen* to *Pan* reflects the old dialect of the Island, compare Black Pan (near Sandown) and Walpan (near Chale) for the same characteristic. The *Le-* in the Domesday spelling represents the French definite article.

Park Farm (near Nettlestone). To be associated with *Park Hill* 1842, and at a much earlier date with 'the lands of Thomas *de Parco*'

THE DICTIONARY

c.1220, *Parke* 1346. As pointed out by Mr C. D. Webster, this is a manorial name, the 13th-century owners known as *de Parco* ('of the park') having also held Park Place at Carisbrooke from which they took their name.

Park Green Farm, Park Place Farm (west of Carisbrooke). Like Great Park and Newpark Farm, both named from the great medieval 'park' or forest which formerly extended over a much larger area than the present Parkhurst Forest, from the River Medina in the east to Newtown in the west. This vast 'park' is first mentioned as *parco regis* 'the king's park' in the Domesday Book of 1086, and is referred to at the beginning of the 13th century as *Parcum* in Latin, then as *le Parke* 1271, *Parke* 1279, *Oldeparke* 1364, *the Parcke* 1551. From Middle English *park* 'an enclosed tract of land set apart for the breeding and hunting of wild animals'.

Parkhurst, Parkhurst Forest (north-west of Newport). *Perkehurst* c.1200, *Parkhurst* 1255, *King's chace of Parkehurste* 1364, *Kings Forest of Parkhurst* 1769. 'The wooded hill in the hunting park', from Old English *hyrst* with Middle English *park* 'an enclosed tract of land for hunting, a chase'. For the medieval 'park' in question, see the previous names. The prison at Parkhurst was established in 1838, the buildings having been taken over from an existing Military Hospital erected in 1799.

Peacock Hill (near Culver Cliff). Self-explanatory.

Pelhamfield (in Ryde). Named after Hon. Charles Anderson *Pelham* later Lord Yarborough, who took a long lease of the area in 1810 before it was developed as a suburb of Ryde.

Pell Farm (in Ryde). Named from the Pell stream, called 'the water at *la Pelle*' c.1290, which runs through Pellhurst Wood. The origin is Old English *pyll* 'a creek or small stream'.

Perreton Farm (near Arreton). *Perytone* 1531, *Peryton alias Pirton* 1608, *Periton* 1769. 'The pear orchard, or the farmstead where pear-trees grow', from Old English *pirige* and *tūn*. The same name occurs as Perton, Pirton, or Purton in several other English counties.

THE PLACE-NAMES OF THE ISLE OF WIGHT

Pidford (near Rookley). *Pideford* c.1290, *Piddeford* 1291, *Pydeford* 1349, *Pidford* 1456. Probably 'the ford in marshy ground', from Old English **pide* and *ford*. The original ford was probably where the road to Sheat Manor from Rookley crosses the two branches of the River Medina.

Pigeon Coo Farm (near Shalfleet). An unusual whimsical name for this farm, formerly called *Grove* as on Andrews's map of 1769, this is probably to be associated with Thomas *atte Grove* 1344, '(living) at the grove or copse', from Old English *grāf*.

Pigtail (near Newbridge). Recorded as *Pyges Tal* in 1559 and as *Pigs Teal* on Andrews's map of 1769. Apparently an allusion to a stream or piece of ground thought to resemble in shape the tail of a pig.

Pilgrims Park (west of Northwood). A modern name, no doubt from a family called *Pilgrim*.

Pitt Place (in Mottistone). *la Putte* 1248, *Pettplace* 1507, *Pett house* 1559, *Pitplace* 1608, *Pitt Place* 1769. 'Residence (Middle English *place*) at Pitt', this being originally 'the pit', from Old English *pytt* 'a pit, a quarry'.

Plaish (near Carisbrooke). *Plaish* 1660, *Plash* 1708, from Old English **plæsc* 'a shallow pool'. The place is on the stream (now Lukely Brook) which gave name to Carisbrooke. It was called *Hill(d)en* 1583, 1608 (origin uncertain).

Pond, The (in Bonchurch). This is shown on an old estate map dating from 1729.

Pondcast Farm (near Havenstreet). Recorded as *Pondcast* in 1662 and as *Poncast* on Andrews's map of 1769. Etymology doubtful.

Pondwell (near Nettlestone). Called *Nettlestone Ponds* in 1663, then *Pownells Fm* on Wright's plan of 1799, *Pondwell's House & Grounds* in 1840, and *Pondwell House* on Weller's map of 1862. From Middle English *ponde* 'a pond or pool'.

THE DICTIONARY

Porchfield (near Locksgreen). *Portsfildes* 1559, *Porchfield* 1769, *Portsfield* 1862. 'Field(s) belonging to the *Port* family', from a local family mentioned in records from the 13th and 14th centuries.

Pound Green (in Freshwater). So called in 1837 and self-explanatory, from *pound* 'enclosure for animals'; the old village pound still remains.

Presford Farm (near Shorwell). *Prestford* 1235, *Presford* 1305, *Prisford* 1306, *Presford* 1769. 'The ford of the priests', from Old English *prēost* and *ford*. The road from Kingston to Shorwell crosses a small stream here.

Preston Farm (in Ryde). *Prestetone* 1086 (Domesday Book), *Prestitun* c.1220, *Prestetune* 13th century, *Prestone* 1378, *Preston* 1428. 'The farmstead or estate belonging to the priests', from Old English *prēost* (genitive plural *prēosta*) and *tūn*, a name found in various other English counties. In medieval times the place was sometimes known as *Preston Vavasour* (as in a document dated 1408), the manorial affix referring to the family of Hugh *Vavassor* c.1220, John *le Vavasour* 1324, who held part of Preston in the 13th and 14th centuries.

Princelett (1½ miles south of Newchurch). *Prunesloude* (probably an error for *Primesfloude*) 1271, *Premsfloude* 1305, *Prymesfloude* 1316, *Prynslode* 1428, *Princelet* 1769. 'The spring belonging to a man called Prim', from Old English *flōde* and an Old English personal name.

Prince's Green (in Cowes). Presented to the town in 1863, no doubt named after the Prince Consort.

Priory (in Carisbrooke). The Dominican Priory here was founded in 1865-6. The site of the medieval Priory at Carisbrooke, the former Alien Benedictine Priory of St Mary, founded c.1156 as a cell of the Abbey of Lyre in Normandy, is now occupied by modern farm buildings to the north of the conventual church, which still survives as the parish church of Carisbrooke.

THE PLACE-NAMES OF THE ISLE OF WIGHT

Priory Bay & The Priory (in Nettlestone). The Priory house (marked as *Priory* on Andrews's map of 1769) was moved to its present site further away from the sea in the late 16th century and largely rebuilt c.1790 by Sir Nash Grose, the famous judge. The name recalls the former Cluniac Priory (founded 1071-86, dissolved 1414) which in medieval times stood adjoining the original church of St Helens, only the tower of which still remains uneroded by the sea (just south of the present house).

Puckaster Cove (near St Catherine's Point). First recorded as *Puckester* 1608, then as *Puckaster Cove* 1769, *Puckester Cove* 1816, *Puckcaster Cove* 1844. Once fancifully considered by antiquarians to represent a corruption of Latin *Port Castra*, but this is highly unlikely. Instead it probably means 'the rock or rocky hill haunted by a goblin', from *puck* (Old English *pūca*) and *torr*, with the later addition of *cove* 'small bay'. Puckwell Farm, just north from here, is recorded as *Pokewell* 1461, 'the spring or stream haunted by a goblin', from the same word *pūca* with Old English *wella*.

Puck House (near Binstead). Near woodland called Puckhouse Copse, earlier Puckers Copse, and to be associated with *Puckes or Puckis Mead* 1653. The first element may be Old English *pūca* 'a goblin' as in the previous name, but perhaps here used as a surname.

Puckpool Point (near Ryde). *Chochepon* (sic) 1086 (Domesday Book), *Cukepole* 1255, *Cokepole* 1287-90, *Cokepoule* 1316, *Puck Pool* 1769, *Puckpool or Popful Point* 1829. Probably 'the pool belonging to a man called Cuca', from Old English *pōl* and an Old English personal name. The Norman spelling of the Domesday Book scribe is rather unusual but does belong here. It will be noted that the curious change from the historically correct *Cuckpool* to the modern form *Puckpool* is relatively recent; for some reason the name must have come to be associated with the word *puck* which is from Old English *pūca* 'a goblin'.

Pyle (near Chale). So named on Andrews's map of 1769, and probably to be associated with Richard *de La Pile* 1255, Walter *atte Pyle* 1320, '(living) at the post or stake' (perhaps one used as a boundary mark), from Old English *pīl*.

THE DICTIONARY

Pyle Street (in Newport). *La Pilstrete* 1293, *Pylestret* 1337. Perhaps to be associated with Margery *de la Pile* c.1270; in any case the origin is Old English *pīl* 'a post or stake' as in the previous name.

Quarr Abbey, Quarr Hill (near Fishbourne). *Quarreria, Quarera* c.1140, *Quadraria* 1142-7, *Quarere* 1166, *Quarr* 1247, *Quarre* 1266, *Quarry Abby* 1769. 'The quarry', from Old French *quarr(i)ere*, latinized in the earliest forms. The original Cistercian Abbey of St Mary, founded in 1132, was named from the stone quarry here, which once supplied the stone used for building the Abbey itself, as well as for numerous other buildings such as Winchester and Chichester Cathedrals. The old Abbey has been in ruins since the 16th century, but the new Abbey here was finished in 1914.

Quarries, The (near Shalcombe). Self-explanatory.

Quay Street (in Newport). *Keystrete* 1504. Self-explanatory, from Middle English *key* 'a quay'.

Queen's Bower (near Newchurch). Recorded as *Queen Bower* on Andrews's map of 1769, and said by some to be named from the 'bower' or arbour Queen Anne (1702-14) had here when she came hawking. However an alternative tradition has it that the place is so called because Isabella de Fortibus, Lady of Wight in the 13th century, had a hunting-box here in what was then the extensive forest of Borthwood.

Rains Grove (1½ miles west of Gatcombe). Recorded as *Rawmes* 1583, *Rawnes* 1615, but as *Rayners Grove* on Worsley's map of 1781. Perhaps from a family name (families called *Rayn* and *Reynor* are mentioned in the 17th-century Hearth Tax returns for Roud and Shorwell respectively), but possibly to be associated with *Reyneris* c.1241, probably 'area of brushwood frequented by female roe-deer or she-goats', from Old English *rǣge* (genitive plural *rǣgena*) and *hrīs*. Two other places in this vicinity are called *Reynecumbe* and *Reynemere* in c.1241, 'the valley and pool frequented by female roe-deer or she-goats', from Old English *cumb* and *mere*.

THE PLACE-NAMES OF THE ISLE OF WIGHT

Ramsdown Farm (near Chillerton). *Romesdone* 1279, *Rammesdone* 1286, *Ramesdon* c.1286, *Ramse Down* 1638, *Ramsdown* 1781. 'The hill of the ram', or 'the hill where wild garlic grows', from Old English *ramm* or *hramsa* and *dūn*.

Rancombe (ruin, near Shorwell). *Ranecumbe* 1227, *Ranecombe* 1299, *Ranecumbe* c.1241, *Rankham* 1759.'The valley frequented by roe-deer', from Old English *rā* (genitive plural *rāna*) and *cumb*.

Red Cliff (near Yaverland). So called on Andrews's map of 1769. Self-explanatory, from the sandstone cliffs here.

Redhill Farm (near Wroxall). *Redehulle* 1454, *le Redhulle, Redhille* 1455, *Redhill* 1781. Self-explanatory, 'the red hill', from Old English *rēad* and *hyll*.

Redway (1 mile south of Arreton). *atterideweie* 1302, *Redway* 1611. Probably 'the way to the reed-bed', from Old English *hrēod* and *weg*. The place is near the River Yar. The first spelling occurs as a surname, with Middle English *atte* representing '(living) at the'. The farm itself was called *Metolls Place alias Spanners* (from families so named) until the 17th century.

Reeth Bay (near St Catherine's Point). Recorded as *Reythe* in 1559, and sometimes represented as *Wreaths or Wraith's Bay* in the early part of this century. Once somewhat fancifully thought to be so called from the *wraiths* of dead bodies washed ashore from shipwrecks (!), but in fact probably from Old English *writha* 'something circular or curved' and therefore descriptive of the shape of the bay.

Rew Down (near Ventnor). *Rowedone* 1285, *Rowdowne* 1550, *Rew Down* 1769, *Rue Down* 1781. Originally 'the rough hill or down', from Old English *rūh* (dative case *rūwan*) and *dūn*, later influenced by nearby Rew Farm which has a quite different origin.

Rew Farm (near Ventnor). *Rewe* 1266, *Rew* 1493, *la Rewe* c.1500, *Rue* 1781. Probably 'the row of trees, the hedgerow', from Old English *ræw*, with the French definite article in the c.1500 form. The

THE DICTIONARY

same name occurs in Devon but there possibly with the meaning 'row of houses'; see next name.

Rew Street (near Northwood). *Rewestret* 14th century, *Rewstreete* 1708, *Rue Street* 1781. 'The street or hamlet with a row of trees or houses', from Old English *rǣw* and *strǣt*; see previous name.

Ridge Copse (near Northwood). *la Rigge* 1342, *Rigge* 1390, *Ridge* 1769. '(The place at) the ridge or bank', from Old English *hrycg*, with the French definite article in the earliest form.

Rill, Lower (near Chillerton). *Rihull* 1290, *Rihille* 1299, *Ryhulle* 1321, *Rill* 1769. 'The hill where rye is grown', from Old English *ryge* and *hyll*. There is another Rill with the same origin and meaning in Newchurch, the earliest spelling being *Ryalle* 1449.

Robin Hill (near Arreton). A modern name, self-explanatory.

Rock (near Brighstone). Recorded as *Hoke* 1565, *Hooke* 1597, but as *Rocks* on Andrews's map of 1769, and possibly to be associated with Mathilda *atte Roke* 1271. Probably '(place) at the oak-tree', from Middle English *atter oke*, the initial *R-* resulting from the misdivision of Middle English *atter* 'at the'. The 16th-century forms suggest confusion with Old English *hōc* 'a hook or angle of land, a bend in a river or road'.

Rocken End (near St Catherine's Point). First recorded as *Rocken End* on Andrews's map of 1769. Although there are no earlier spellings, the meaning may be 'end of the rocks, rocky promontory', with *-en* representing an old dialect plural. Alternatively *Rocken* may be a reduced form of an earlier *Rock End*, to which a further 'explanatory' *End* was later added.

Rodge Brook (flowing through Porchfield into Newtown Bay). *Rachebroke* 1235, *Rachebrok* 1299, *Racchebrooke* 1476, *Rodgebrook* 1769. Probably 'the brook of the hunting-dogs', from Old English *ræcc* and *brōc*.

THE PLACE-NAMES OF THE ISLE OF WIGHT

Rookley, Rookley Green (2 miles north-west of Godshill). *Roclee* 1202, *Rokele* 1235, *Roukley* 1328, *Rookeley* 1583, *Rookley (Green)* 1769. 'The wood or woodland clearing frequented by rooks', from Old English *hrōc* and *lēah*.

Roslin (near Chillerton). *Rossling* 1608, *Roseland* 1708, *Rossland* 1759. Possibly a manorial name indicating lands formerly possessed by a family called *Roslin(g)*.

Roud (near Godshill). *Rode* 1086 (Domesday Book), *Rud* 1248, *Roude* 1287-90, *Rowde* 1428. Probably '(place at) the reed-bed', from Old English *hrēod*. The place is situated near the River Yar. Rowde in Wiltshire has the same origin.

Round Tower Point (on coast south-west of Sconce Point). Named after *Worseleys tower* 1583, *Worsleys Towre* 1611, an outlook tower built by Sir James Worsley (died 1538) but now demolished.

Rowborough Down & Farm (1 mile north of Shorwell). *Rowebere* 1272-9, *Rougheberg* 1282, *Rouwebergh* 1284, *Ruheburg* 1289, *Ruberghe* 1424. 'The rough hill', from Old English *rūh* (dative case *rūwan*) and *beorg*.

Rowborough Farm (1 mile north of Brading). *Rodeberge* (sic) 1086 (Domesday Book), *Rouberge* 1277, *Roughburgh* 1346, *Rouburgh* 1436, *Roubury* 1769. Identical in origin with the previous name. The Domesday spelling is an error for *Rogeberge*.

Rowlands Farm & Wood (south of Havenstreet). *Rowlands* 1608, *Rowland(s)* 1664. So called from Robert *Rowland*, tenant here in 1560.

Rowridge (near Calbourne). *Ruwerigge* 1227, *Rurigge* c.1241, *Roweruge* 1251, *Rogherigge* 1335, *Rowrigge* 1431. 'The rough ridge', from Old English *rūh* (dative case *rūwan*) and *hrycg*.

Ruffins Copse (in Northwood). Named after the local family called *Ruffin*: a Dorothy *Ruffin* is mentioned in the 1664 Hearth Tax return under Newport, and members of the same family owned the adjoining farm of Cockleton in the 17th and 18th centuries.

THE DICTIONARY

Run, The (in Bembridge). From the word *run* in the sense 'a flow or current of water, a strong rush of the tide', applied here to a narrow channel between the offshore ledges of rock.

Ryde (3 miles north-west of St Helens). *la Ride* 1257, *Ride* 1265, *la Ryde* 1274, *Rythe* 1420, *Ryde* 1431. '(Place at) the small stream', from Old English *rīth*.

Ryde East Sands (off Ryde). Referred to as *Sande hed* 'the sandy headland' on a British Library map of 1550.

Ryde House (near Ryde). Called *Ride Farm* on Andrews's map of 1769.

Sainham Farm (near Godshill). *Sanham-fielde* 1606, *Saynham field* 1607, *Sainham* 1632, *Seaham* 1759. In spite of the late spellings, possibly 'the homestead or enclosure of a man called Sǣwine', from Old English *hām* or *hamm* and an Old English personal name. Someone with this name held land at nearby Roud in 1086 (Domesday Book).

St Boniface Down (near Bonchurch). Called *Boniface Down* on Andrews's map of 1769, *St Boniface Down* on Worsley's map of 1781, earlier referred to as *Mons Sancti Bonefacii* in a Latin text from the 13th century. Named from the dedication of the Norman church in the neighbouring parish of Bonchurch. The summit of the Down reaches 787 feet, the highest point in the Island.

St Catherine's Down, Hill, & Point (near Chale). (Land called) *Seynt Kateryns* c.1440, *St Katherins hill* 1583, *St Caterine hill* 1595, *St Catherines hill* 1769. All named from 'St Catherine's Oratory', a former chapel-cum-lighthouse dedicated to St Catherine. It was originally founded in 1323 for a priest to say masses for the souls lost at sea and to provide a light to guide seagoing vessels. The chapel itself has disappeared, but the lighthouse remains, known locally as 'the Pepperpot'. The old name has now been transferred to the new lighthouse built in 1840 at St Catherine's Point. St Catherine's Down (781 feet at its summit, the second highest point in the Island) was

89

THE PLACE-NAMES OF THE ISLE OF WIGHT

formerly *Chaledone* 1324, *Chaledowne* 1520, that is 'the down near Chale'; it was the site of a defensive beacon in 1324.

St George's Down (near Arreton). So called on Andrews's map of 1769. Named from the dedication of St George's church at Arreton. The earlier name of St George's Down was no doubt *Stāndūn* 'the stony hill', this being transferred at an early date to the settlements now called Standen.

St Helens (medieval parish, near Bembridge). *Sancta Elena* 12th century, *Seynt Eleyne* 1279, *Seyntelenes* 1418, *Seint Ellyns* 1544. Named from the dedication of the church to St Helena. All that remains of the original church, built in the 12th century and once attached to a Cluniac priory, is the tower, which still stands on the shore to the east of the village and is used as a sea-mark. The rest of the building was eroded away by the sea, and the present church of St Helens was built a mile inland to replace it. The Domesday Book (1086) manor of *Etharin* is possibly to be identified with St Helens. This name may represent an Old English *æt harum* '(place) at the cairns or heaps of stones', from the dative plural case of Old English **hær* 'rock, heap of stones, tumulus' preceded by the preposition *æt*. Moreover in medieval times (from at least as early as the 12th century) the village of St Helens was sometimes called Eddington, a manor recorded as *Edynetone* 1104, c.1240, that is probably 'the farmstead or estate belonging to a woman called Ēadwynn', from Old English *tūn* and an Old English personal name.

St John's Park (in Ryde). Named from *St John's House*, a mansion built in the 18th century and called after the town of St John's in Newfoundland, capital of that province and the first English settlement in Canada.

St Lawrence (medieval parish, 2 miles west of Ventnor). *Sancti Laurencii* 1255, *St. Laurence Wa* 1297, *Wathe* 1311, *St Laurence de Wathe* 1340. Named from the dedication of the church to St Lawrence, but the place was originally also known as *Wathe*, '(the place at) the ford', from Old English *wæd*. Indeed, as Mr C. D. Webster points out, the name *Wathe* was often used to denote the whole area of the Undercliff from Bonchurch to Niton, one part of it

THE DICTIONARY

(in the manor of Whitwell) being called *Southwathe* 1287-90 or *Stoureswath* 1292 (because it belonged to the *Estur* family), and another *Underwathe* 1250-60, '(the place) below *Wathe*'. The name *Wathe* was in fact still in use up until the 17th century, although the ford referred to, situated north-east of the village, has long since disappeared together with the small stream on which it stood. The old church of St Lawrence, until 1842 the smallest parish church in England, is said to date from 1197.

St Martin's Down (near Wroxall). *Smerdone* c.1240, *Smeredon* 1274, *la Smeredone* 1276, *Smerdon down* 1464, *Smarden Barn* 1769, *Smar Down* 1781. 'The hill or down where butter is produced' (i.e. with rich pasture), from Old English *smeoru* and *dūn*. The recent transformation of the name through folk etymology, or sound similarity, is remarkable: obviously the first part of *Smardon Down* (with the second addition of *Down* in fact strictly tautological) has been imaginatively reinterpreted as *St Martin* – a spurious saint indeed!

Saltern Wood (near Norton) A *Saltern* is marked near here on Andrews's map of 1769. From Old English *salt-ærn* 'a building where salt is made or sold'. Salt was no doubt produced in this area near the mouth of the River Yar in medieval times.

Samber Hill (1 mile south of Shorwell). Probably to be associated with *Sanberghe* 1235, 'the sandy hill', from Old English *sand* and *beorg*.

Sandford (near Godshill). *Sandford* 1086 (Domesday Book), *Saunford* 1279, *Sandforde* 15th century, *Sanforde* 1552. 'The sandy ford' from Old English *sand* and *ford*. The Domesday spelling, remarkably enough unchanged in over 900 years, appears in documents throughout the centuries.

Sandhills Farm (near Locksgreen). *Saddehella* (sic) 12th century, *Sandhulle* 1248, *Sondihulle* 1251, *la Sandihulle* 1254, *Sandhilles* 1608. 'The sand(y) hill', from Old English *sand* (noun) alternating with *sandig* (adjective) and *hyll*. The addition of final -*s* seems only to date from the 17th century.

Sandown (1½ miles north of Shanklin). *Sande* (sic) 1086 (Domesday Book), *Sandome* 1204, *Sandham* 1271, *Sandeham* 1327, *Sandam* 1432, *Sanden* 1520, *Sandown* 1759. 'The sandy enclosure or river-meadow', from Old English *sand* and *hamm*. The Domesday spelling may be simply erratic, with the omission of *-ham*, but it could represent an Old English **sænde* meaning 'sandy place'. It will be noted that the relatively recent modern spelling is quite unhistorical, the weakened pronunciation of the second part of the name having been understood as a reduction of the word *down*. In medieval times the manor was divided into two, appearing in the records as *Southsandham* (the area now called Lake) and *Northsandham* (modern Sandown) in the 13th to 16th centuries. A castle for the defence of the coast built here by Henry VIII in 1546 is marked on a map of 1595 as *Sandham castle*, this being replaced by another built about 1632 called *Sandham or Sandown Fort* on Andrews's map of 1769. The first of these was situated too near the shore and was encroached upon by the sea, the second was demolished at the beginning of this century.

Sandown Bay (off Sandown). *Sandham bay* 1583, *Sandam baye* 1591, *Sandome bay* 1611, *Sandown Bay* 1781. See previous entry.

Sandy Way (in Shorwell). So called in 1735, self-explanatory; see Samber Hill in the same parish.

School Green (in Freshwater). Called *School house Green* in 1837, and named from the village green (*Freshwater Green* on Andrews's map of 1769) near to which the first school in the district once stood.

Sconce Point (on coast west of Yarmouth). So called on Avery's map of 1720, named from *Sconce Fort* 1700, *Carey's Sconce* 1769, the *sconce* (meaning 'a small fort') being one built in 1585 (during the reign of Queen Elizabeth I) by Sir George Carey. The earlier name of Sconce Point was *Scharpenorde* 1324, *Sharpnose* 1550, *Sharpnode* 1583, 'the sharp point or promontory' from Old English *scearp* (dative case *scearpan*) and *ord*; this was the site of a beacon in 1324. The latest occurrence of this older name is on Speed's map of 1611, where *Carey's Sconce* is called *Sharpnor castle*.

THE DICTIONARY

Scotchells Brook (a tributary of the 'eastern' River Yar). This preserves the old name *Scaldeford* 1086 (Domesday Book), *Scaudeford* 1271, *Scottesford* 1287-90, *Scotesfield* 17th century, 'the shallow ford', from Old English *sceald* and *ford*. The brook itself takes its name from the ford, which was probably where the road from Sandown to Arreton crosses the brook near Merrie Gardens.

Scotland Corner (in Godshill). Like nearby Scotland Farm, named from *Skotland* 1371, *Skotlandiscroft* 1404, *Scotland* 1608, 'land subject to a particular payment or tax', from Middle English *scot* and *land*. The same name occurs in Devon.

Scratchell's Bay (near The Needles). So called in 1736, spelt *Scratchels Bay* on Andrews's map of 1769, and probably containing the dialect word *Scratch* 'the Devil'. The downland ridge that terminates at The Needles may well have been called *Scratch-hill* (later *Scratchell*) 'the hill of the Devil' on account of the numerous shipwrecks caused by this dangerous coast. It is perhaps no coincidence that Old Harry, the complementary chalk-stack off the coast of Dorset across the water from The Needles, is called after another familiar name for the Devil!

Seagrove Bay (in Nettlestone). Named from Seagrove (recorded as *Sea Grove House, Sea Grove Coppice* 1840), a self-explanatory modern name for 'a grove or copse by the sea'.

Seaview (near Nettlestone). A modern self-explanatory name, first appearing as *Sea View* on Wallis's map of 1839. The place commands a wide outlook over the Solent and the open sea.

Shalcombe (1 mile north of Brook). *Eseldecombe* 1086 (Domesday Book), *Scaldecumbe* 1142-7, *Eschaldecumbe* 1155-61, *Shaldecumb* 1284, *Shalcome* 1526. 'The shallow valley', from Old English *sceald* and *cumb*. The Domesday and mid-12th-century spellings are not uncharacteristic of the Norman scribes; compare modern French words like *espace* 'space' and *esprit* 'spirit'.

Shalfleet (medieval parish, near Newtown). *æt Scealdan fleote* 838 (in a 12th-century copy of a Saxon charter), *Seldeflet* 1086

THE PLACE-NAMES OF THE ISLE OF WIGHT

(Domesday Book), *Schaldflete* 1141-2, *Scaldeflet* 1189-1204, *Shalflete* 1397. '(Place at) the shallow stream or creek', from Old English *sceald* (dative case *scealdan*) and *flēot*. The place takes its name from the narrow creek just north of the village into which flows the stream known as Caul Bourne. The mainly Norman St Michael's Church at Shalfleet stands on the site of an even earlier church mentioned in the Domesday Book of 1086.

Shamblers Copse (in Cowes). Preserves the name of the ancient estate called *Shamelord*, for which see Cowes.

Shanklin (medieval parish, 1½ miles south of Sandown). *Sencliz, Selins* 1086 (Domesday Book), *Shenclyng* 1305, *Shenclyn* 1503, *Chynklyn* 1550, *Shanklin* 1611. 'The bank by the drinking cup' (referring to the waterfall or cascade in the famous Chine), from Old English *scenc* and *hlinc*. The cascade of fresh water must have received its nickname 'the *scenc* or drinking cup' at an early date.

Shanklin Chine & Down (near Shanklin). Both are so named on Andrews's map of 1769. The former is first recorded as *Chynklyng Chyne* on a map of 1550 in the British Library. Chine derives from the Old English word *cinu* 'a ravine'.

Shate Farm (near Brighstone). *Soete* 1086 (Domesday Book), *Sete* 1141-3, *Sieta* c.1200, *Shute* 1255, *Schete* 1280. 'The corner, nook, or angle of land', from Old English **sciēte*. In spite of the difference in the modern spelling, this is thus a doublet of the next name.

Sheat Manor (near Gatcombe). *Essvete* 1086 (Domesday Book), *la Siete* c.1217, *Shete* 1279, *Shute* 1292, *La Shete* 1314, *Sheat* 1769. Identical in origin with Shate Farm. Here the Domesday spelling shows similar Norman characteristics to that of Shalcombe. Carisbrooke Priory had a grange here in medieval times, referred to as *grangiam de la Schete* in c.1220.

Sheepwash Farm (1 mile south of Godshill). *le Shepewashe* 1588, *Sheepwash* 1769, *Shipwash* 1785. Self-explanatory, from Old English *scēap-wæsce* 'a place for dipping sheep'. The spelling from the 1785 map reflects the local pronunciation. There are at least four other

THE DICTIONARY

places called Sheepwash on the Island, in Carisbrooke, Freshwater, Northwood and Whippingham, confirming the importance of sheep in the local economy since early times.

Sheepwash Green (in Freshwater). *Sheep Wash Green* in 1837, identical in origin with the previous name.

Shepherd's Chine (near Brighstone Bay). Probably self-explanatory, 'the chine of the shepherd'. It gives name to the long distance trail known as 'Shepherd's Trail'. At an earlier date it was called *Kingetts Chine* 1630, from the local *Kingett* family who held two tenements in the Chine.

Shide (in Newport). *Side, Sida* 1086 (Domesday Book), *Side* 1189-1204, *Schida* c.1230, *Shide* 1250-60, *Shyde* 1387, *Shide Bridge & Mill* 1769. '(Place at) the plank or foot-bridge', from Old English *scīd*. The first bridge here over the River Medina may well have been no more than a plank or beam of wood. A bridge is actually mentioned in the 13th century as *pontem de ssyde* (that is 'the bridge of Shide') and as *Schidhambrigge* ('the bridge at the Shide river-meadow', from Old English *hamm*).

Shippards Chine (near Brook). Probably from the word *shepherd*, thus identical in origin with Shepherd's Chine in Brighstone in spite of the different spelling.

Shorwell (medieval parish, 1½ miles east of Brighstone). *Sorewelle* 1086 (Domesday Book), *Sorewell* 1141-3, *Shorewell* 1220, *Schorwell* 1227, *Shorwelle* 1255. 'The spring or stream by the steep slope', from Old English *scora* and *wella*. The name refers to the situation of the village in a deep valley at the foot of the downs. The stream rising here (at a spring called Shor Well in the grounds of North Court manor) flows into the sea at Grange Chine in Brighstone.

Shute, The (in Whitwell). Near St Lawrence Shute, both containing the old dialect word *shute* (from Old English *scyte*) meaning 'a steep hill in a road or lane'.

THE PLACE-NAMES OF THE ISLE OF WIGHT

Sibdown (near Rookley). *Sipedone, Cippedone* c.1248, *Sypedone* c.1300, *Sipedon* 1324, *Sybedone* 1402, *Sibdown* 1769. Possibly 'the hill or down near the marshy pool', from an Old English word **sipe* and *dūn*.

Skinners Farm (near Northwood). To be associated with *Skinners Grove* 1708. Probably a manorial name, indicating lands formerly held here by a family called *Skinner*; a *grove* is 'a small copse'.

Smallbrook Farm (south of Ryde). *Smalbroke* 1251, *Smalebroke* c.1260, *Smalbrok* 1305, *Smalbrook* 1385, *(Little) Small Brook* 1769. 'The narrow brook', from Old English *smæl* and *brōc*. The brook is now called Monktonmead Brook, which is named from *Monken Meade* 1544, 'the meadow of the monks'.

Smallmoor (near Shorwell). Recorded as *Smallmoore* 1571 and as *Small more* on Andrews's map of 1769. 'The narrow marsh', from Old English *smæl* and *mōr*.

Smithclose (near Wootton Bridge). Possibly to be associated with Smythers Hill Copse which is named from *Smitheswelle* c.1224, 'the spring or stream of the smith'.

Smuggler's Path (in Bonchurch). A track in the Lower Landslip, a reminder that smuggling was rife along this stretch of coast in the old days.

Solent, The (the sea channel between the Island and the mainland). An ancient pre-English name of uncertain origin and meaning, first recorded as *Soluente* 731, later as *le Soland* 1395.

Somerton Farm (in Northwood). *Somertone* 1316, *Summerton* 1694, *Sumerton* 1704, *Somerton* 1769. 'The farmstead used mainly or only in summer', from Old English *sumor* and *tūn*. The same name occurs in Oxfordshire and Somerset.

Southford (near Whitwell). First recorded as *Southford* in 1632, 'the south ford' from Old English *sūth* and *ford*, so called to distinguish it from *Northford* which is the present Ford Farm.

THE DICTIONARY

South Street (in Newport). An old street-name, first recorded as *Suthstrete* in the 13th century. Self-explanatory.

Span Farm (near Wroxall). *Spanne* c.1280, *La Spanne* 1287-90, *Spanne* c.1300, *Span* 1769. From Old English *spann* 'a span, a hand's breadth', used either of 'a narrow strip of land' or of 'a foot-bridge spanning a stream'.

Spithead (the sea channel between the Island and Portsmouth). Not recorded before 1629, 'the headland of the sand-spit or pointed sandbank', from Old English *spitu* and *hēafod*. The sand-spit which gave the channel its name lies off Gosport and is still called Spit Sand or Spit Bank.

Spring Copse (near St Helens). So called in 1842 and self-explanatory, 'the coppice wood with a spring'.

Springhill (in East Cowes). A self-explanatory modern name, 'the hill with a spring'.

Spring Vale (near Nettlestone). Self-explanatory, 'the valley with a spring'.

Stag Rock (near The Needles). A pyramid-shaped rock which once formed part of the cliff. A colourful but perhaps not impossible legend has it that it owes its name to the fact that a stag, pursued by hounds, leapt on to it from the adjacent cliff at a time before the present degree of erosion had taken place.

Stagwell (1 mile south-west of Northwood). *Stackell* (a field) 1608, *Stagwell* 1708, *Stockwell or Stock Grove* 1769, *Stugwell* 1844. Probably 'the spring or stream marked by a boundary post', from Old English *staca* and *wella*. The stream just west of Stagwell seems to be one mentioned as *tha wylle* 'the spring or steam' in a 10th-century survey of the bounds of Watchingwell.

Standen House, Little East Standen Farm, Great East Standen Manor (east of Arreton). *Standone* (twice) 1086 (Domesday Book), *Staundon* 1248, *Westaundene* 1271, *Estaundone* 1289, *Great & Little*

Standen, Standen (Farm) 1769. 'The stony hill or down', from Old English *stān* and *dūn*, this being originally the name of what is now called St George's Down before it was transferred to the two manors called *Standone* in Domesday Book. These were later to be distinguished as East and West Standen (the latter now represented by Standen House, which dates back to 1690).

Staplers, Staplers Farm (east of Newport). *Stapelhurst* 1235, *Staplehirst* c.1250, *Stapelherst* c.1300, *Staplurste* 1608, *Staplers (Heath)* 1769. 'The wooded hill where posts are obtained', from Old English *stapol* and *hyrst*. Staplehurst in Kent has the same origin. Staplers Farm is probably the site of a medieval grange belonging to Quarr Abbey.

Steel Bay (near Dunnose). Not in the early records, but more than likely from Old English *stigel* 'a steep ascent'.

Steephill, Steep Hill Cove (near Ventnor). *Stupele* 1316, *Steple* 1586, *Steeple* 1769, *Steephill* 1781. 'The steep place', from Old English *stīepel*. The second syllable of the word has been interpreted in modern times as if it was the word *hill*. The 'regular' development would have been to Steeple, which is the modern spelling of names with the same origin in Dorset and Essex.

Stenbury Down, Stenbury Manor Farm (near Whitwell). *Staneberie* 1086 (Domesday Book), *la Steniberi* 1189-1204, *Stenebire* 1235, *Steynebery* 1299, *La Stenenbury* 1305. 'The stone-built fortified place', from Old English *stænen* (adjective) 'made of stone' and *burh* (dative case *byrig*) 'fort'. The Jacobean manor house here stands on the site of an earlier moated dwelling dating back to the 13th century: this in turn may have been the site of the earlier *burh*. Stenbury Down is so called on Worsley's map of 1781. It gives name to the long distance trail known as 'Stenbury Trail'.

Steyne Cross, Steyne House (in Bembridge). Appearing as *Stane* on Andrews's map of 1769, and as *Steyne Villa* on Nichols's map of 1844, but the name is mistakenly written *Spain* (an error for *Stain*) on Wright's map of 1799 and other 19th-century maps. An earlier reference is to (land called) *Schortstene* in the early 14th century, establishing that the origin is Old English *stæne* 'a stony place' as is

THE DICTIONARY

the case with another Steyne (*la Stene* c.1290) in Chale. Steyne Cross contains *cross* in the sense 'cross-roads'.

Sticelett (near Northwood). *stithes fleotes heafod* 968 (in a 13th-century copy of a Saxon charter), *Stithesflet* late 13th century, *Stysslede* 1548, *Sticelett* 1708. Probably 'the shallow stream or creek of a man called *Stīth', from Old English *flēot* and an Old English personal name. The early spelling (meaning 'the head or source of Stīth's stream') occurs in a 10th-century survey of the bounds of Watchingwell. The stream in question is that flowing into the sea at Thorness Bay.

Stickworth Hall (Hotel, near Arreton). So called on Albin's map of 1823, but apparently called *Stickworth Grove House* when rebuilt in 1793. Named from a messuage called *Stickworths* in 1562 and therefore possibly from a family name, but origin uncertain without earlier spellings.

Stone Farm (near Blackwater). *atte Stone* 1327, *La Stone* 1391, *Stone* 1559. '(Place at) the stone', from Old English *stān*, originally perhaps with reference to a standing stone or boundary stone. The earliest spelling occurs as the surname of someone living here 'at the stone'.

Stone Place Farm (in Shorwell). *Stone Place* 1780. Probably self-explanatory, 'stone-built mansion', but compare the previous name.

Stoneshell (south-east of Newchurch). Marked as simply *Stone* on Andrews's map of 1769, but otherwise *Stondhull* c.1327, *Stondhill* 1467, *Stoneshill* 1582, *Stoneshull* 1831, *Stone Shell* 1852. 'The stone hill', or rather 'the hill at the stone', from Old English *stān* and *hyll*. It is possible that the 'stone' that gave rise to the name is the one referred to as *thone stan* 'the (boundary) stone' in the Saxon bounds of Bathingbourne (c.953).

Stonesteps (north of Calbourne). Called *Stone Steps* on Andrews's map of 1769, *Stoney Steps* on Worsley's map of 1781. Self-explanatory.

THE PLACE-NAMES OF THE ISLE OF WIGHT

Strathwell Park (near Whitwell). The Victorian Gothic house so called was built by Mr Oliver, vicar of Whitwell, on the site of a tenement earlier known as *Strattle* 1596, and still recorded thus on Andrews's map of 1769. Without earlier spellings its origin and meaning must remain obscure.

Sugar Loaf (near St Catherine's Point). A prominent cliff knoll overhanging the sea, so called from its shape.

Summersbury (near Godshill). *Somerisbourgh* 1291, *Somersburgh, Someresburghe* 1349, *Somerborough* 1447, *Sommers Barrowe* 1571, *Summersbury* 1769. Possibly 'the hill with pastures used mainly in summer', from Old English *sumor* and *beorg*. Alternatively, 'the hill of a man called *Sumor', if the first element is an Old English personal name.

Sun Corner (near The Needles). An appropriate name for this south-east facing promontory overlooking Scratchell's Bay.

Sutton Farm (near Brighstone). *Suthetone* 1248, *Suthintone* 1271, *Sudinton* 1278, *Suttone* 1283, *Suttons* 1769. '(The place) south of the estate or village', from Old English *sūthan* and *tūn*. The place is no doubt named in relation to Brighstone.

Swains Farm & Lane (in Bembridge). *Swaynes* 1632, *Swains Fm* 1799. Named after Geoffrey *Swain* and Margery his wife who held land here c.1280. The surname derives from the Old Scandinavian personal name *Sveinn* found in Swainston.

Swainston (1 mile north-east of Calbourne). *Sweineston* 1213, *Swenestone* 1220, *Sweyneston* 1251, *Swayneston* 1285. 'The farmstead or estate belonging to a man called Sveinn', from Old English *tūn* and an Old Scandinavian personal name. The name *Sveinn* was first introduced into England by the Vikings, but was also in use among the Normans, so it is likely that this early owner of the estate was of Viking or Norman stock; the name occurs as both first name and surname on the Island in medieval times.

THE DICTIONARY

Swanmore (near Ryde). So named c.1850 by Bettesworth Pitts Shearer from Swanmore in Hampshire, who called this portion of his Ashey estate on the outskirts of Ryde after his former home. Swanmore in Hampshire was originally *Swanemere*, 'pool of the swans', from Old English *swan* and *mere*.

Swiss Cottage (near Osborne). A building in the style of a Swiss chalet, originally built as a 'play-house' for Queen Victoria's children in 1854 during their residence at Osborne House. There are other houses with the same name in Arreton and Carisbrooke.

Tapnell Farm (1 mile south of Thorley). Recorded as *Tapnel Farm* in 1755 and as *Tapnel* on Andrews's map of 1769. Without earlier spellings, the origin and meaning of the name must remain obscure.

Tennyson Down (near Freshwater Bay). Formerly called *High Down* (as on Andrews's map of 1769), but now so called because of the gift in 1927, by the Lord Tennyson to the National Trust in memory of his father the Poet Laureate, of part of the Down around the Tennyson Cross. The Cross itself, dating from 1897, celebrates the fact that Alfred Lord Tennyson, who lived at Farringford House, liked to sit here gazing out to sea.

Thorley (medieval parish, near Yarmouth), **Thorley Street**. *Torlei* 1086 (Domesday Book), *Thornlega* 1185, *Thornle* 1292, *Thorley* 1334, *Thurley* 1550. 'The thorn-tree wood or clearing', from Old English *thorn* and *lēah*. The word *street* is used here in the sense 'street of houses, hamlet'. There is another Thorley with the same origin in Hertfordshire.

Thorley Brook (near Thorley). Referred to as simply *le Brouke* in 1295, 'the brook', from Old English *brōc*.

Thorncross (near Brighstone). Earlier called *Thorners* 1508 or *Thornplace* 1559, but recorded as *Turn Cross* on Andrews's map of 1769. Probably self-explanatory, 'the cross-roads near thorn-trees', from *thorn* and *cross*.

THE PLACE-NAMES OF THE ISLE OF WIGHT

Thorness Bay, Great & Little Thorness (west of Northwood). *Torneyam* 1198-1216, *Thorneye* 1285, *Thornheye* 1324, *Thornesbay* 1395, *Thorney Bay, Great & Little Thorney* 1769, *Thorness Bay, Great & Little Thorness* 1781. Originally 'the thorn-tree hedge or enclosure', from Old English *thorn* and *hege* or *hæg*. *Thorne(y)sbay* (representing 'the bay at *Thorney*') then developed to *Thorness (Bay)* through confusion with a different word *ness* from Old English *næss* 'headland'.

Three Gates Farm (1 mile east of Shalfleet). Apparently self-explanatory, but according to Mr C. D. Webster called *Thre Croughts* in 1560, this perhaps representing 'three crofts' with an inverted spelling for *croft* (compare the spellings of words like *draught* and *laughter*).

Totland (near Freshwater). *Toteland* c.1240, *Tottelonde* 1337, *Toteland* 1341, *Totland* 1608. 'The cultivated land or estate with a look-out place', from Old English **tōt* and *land*. The look-out would have used a beacon to warn of danger, and there is in fact mention of a beacon on Headon Hill in Totland as early as 1324. The name Warden Point in Totland also makes reference to keeping watch.

Totland Bay (near Totland). First so called on Avery's map of 1720.

Town Copse (near Newtown). Named from its proximity to Newtown.

Tyne Hall (in Bembridge). *Tyne* 15th century, *Tyen* 1632. 'The small enclosures', from Old English *tēag*, this word occurring here in a Middle English plural form with *-en*. In the 14th and 15th century one of the enclosures was called *Swenesstye*, 'enclosure of a family called *Swene* or *Swain*'. The same family gave name to the nearby Swains Farm.

Undercliff, The (along the coast between St Catherine's Point and Ventnor). Recorded as *under le Cliffe* 1608, *under Clift* 1771, '(the ground) under the cliff', from Old English *under* and *clif*. At an earlier date perhaps called *Underwathe*, for which see St Lawrence.

THE DICTIONARY

Undercliff, The (along the coast between Brook and Brighstone). Identical in origin with the previous name.

Under Tyne (in Bembridge). One of the beaches here, meaning 'below Tyne', with reference to Tyne Hall.

Upper Hyde (near Shanklin), see Hyde.

Upton (near Havenstreet). Recorded as *Upton* 1560, *Uptoune* 1650, and as *Upton* on Andrews's map of 1769 (with a complementary *Low Town* to the north-west). Probably an old name meaning 'the higher farmstead', from Old English *upp* and *tūn*.

Valleys (in Carisbrooke). Named after Richard *Valley*, who inherited this property in 1616.

Vayres Farm (near Carisbrooke). *Veyres Lond* 1537, *Veyres* 1560, *Veares* 1781, *Vaeres* 1812. Named after the *Vere* or *Veer* family who are mentioned in 15th-century records.

Ventnor (2 miles south of Shanklin). Recorded as *Vintner* 1591, *Vyntnor* 1607, *(farm of) Vintner* 1617, *messuage or tenement called Vintner or Vintners* 1633, then with its present spelling from 1769. Probably a manorial name, indicating an estate formerly held by a family called *Vintner*. The surname *Vintner* derives from a Middle English word *vintener* (from Old French *vintenier*) meaning 'lieutenant, military officer in command of twenty men'. In medieval times the Island was divided into nine districts for its military defence, with a *vintener* appointed to be in charge of each district. The term often occurs in the local records, e.g. as the occupation of William *le Vyntener*, one of the four jurors appointed to supervise the collection of taxes in Bonchurch in 1341. The old name of Ventnor was *Holeweia* 1189-1204, *Holeweye* 1287-90, *Holloway* 1553, that is 'the hollow way, or the way in a hollow', from Old English *hol* and *weg*, referring to the road running north out of Ventnor between Rew Down and St Boniface Down.

Vittlefield(s) Farm (1½ miles north-west of Carisbrooke). *Fithelyfeld* 1298, *Fythilifeld* 1299, *Fithelfeld* 1364, *Vittlefeildes* 1608,

THE PLACE-NAMES OF THE ISLE OF WIGHT

Wittlefields 1769. The second element is Old English *feld* 'open land', the first is uncertain in spite of the fairly early spellings. It is just possible that it is Old English **fitheling* 'playing the fiddle', giving a sense 'open land where fiddles are played', perhaps a reference to feasting or merrymaking here; in this case Wakefield in Yorkshire, which means 'open land where festivals take place', might be compared. Alternatively the first element may contain an Old English plant-name **fithele* in the form **fitheling* 'place where this plant grows'.

Wackland (near Newchurch). *Wakelonde, Wakelande* 1249, *Wakelond* 1287-90, *Wackelond* 1311, *Waklond* 1431. 'The cultivated land or estate where a watch is kept', from Old English **wacu* and *land*. The meaning is thus similar to that of Totland. It is interesting to note that Speed's map of 1611 marks the site of a beacon here.

Walpan (near Chale). *Valpenne* 1086 (Domesday Book), *Walepen* 12th century, *Walepanne* c.1240, *Walpanne* 1302, *Walpan* 1428. The second element is Old English *penn* 'a pen or fold for animals', with its characteristic dialect form *pann* as in (Great) Pan (in Newport) and Black Pan (near Sandown). The first element is less certain, but the most likely is Old English *walu* 'a ridge or embankment' (perhaps referring to the high ground to the north of Walpan). Walpan Chine is marked on Andrews's map of 1769.

Warden Point (near Totland). *Woorden* 1591, *Worden* 1595, *Warden* 1611. 'The watch or look-out hill', from Old English *weard* and *dūn*. The same name occurs in several other English counties. It might be noted that the name Totland also refers to keeping watch at this western extremity of the Island.

Warlands (in Shalfleet). *Wareland* 1559, *capital messuage called Waleron Trenchards* 1617, *Warlands* 1793. A manorial name from a possessive form of the personal name *Waleran*; the Trenchards were the lords of Shalfleet, and in a document dated 1230-40 a farm at *Hiestningewede* (that is 'East Ningwood') was given by Henry Trenchard to his younger son Waleran who in turn granted part of it to the monks of Carisbrooke.

THE DICTIONARY

Warren Farm (near Totland). Called *Warren House* on Andrews's map of 1769. Named from Headon Warren.

Watchingwell, Lower & Upper (2 miles north-east of Calbourne). *Hwætinc, Hwætincg le* 968 (in a 13th-century copy of a Saxon charter), *Watingewelle* 1086 (Domesday Book), *Whatingewelle* 1255, *Watchyngwell* 1559, *Lower & Upper Watchingwell* 1769. 'The spring or stream at the place where wheat is grown', from Old English *hwǣte, -ing* and *wella*. *Hwætinc(g)* 'the wheat place' seems originally to have been the name of the district, to which *wella* 'spring, stream', and earlier *lēah* 'woodland clearing', were added.

Watershoot Bay (near St Catherine's Point). Called *Watershoot Cove* on Norie's chart of 1816, from *watershoot* 'a place where water gushes out', no doubt referring here to water draining from the cliffs into the sea, possibly from a spring like Sandrock Spring some ½ mile up the coast towards Chale Bay.

Waytes Court (in Brighstone). *Waitcourt* 1611, *Weats Court* 1769, *Wait Court* 1781. The building is 17th century in date, but the name is to be associated with the *le Wayte* family who had lands in Brighstone as early as the 14th century. The word *court* has the sense 'large house, manor'.

Weards Cottage (in Niton). Recorded as *Ward's* 1771, and probably preserving an old name *la Wirdde* 1324, from Old English **wierde* 'a watch or look-out'; this was in fact listed as the site of a beacon in 1324.

Wedge Rock (near The Needles). An offshore chalk rock, so called from its shape.

Week Down (near St Lawrence). *Wyke Downe* 1449, *Week Down* 1781. 'The hill or down near Week', from Old English *dūn*; see next name.

Week Farm (near St Lawrence). *Wica* 1086 (Domesday Book), *la Wike* 1189-1204, *Wicha* c.1200, *Wyke* 1248, *Weeke* 1611. 'The specialized farm' (probably a dairy farm), from Old English *wīc*.

THE PLACE-NAMES OF THE ISLE OF WIGHT

There are other places with this name in Cornwall, Hampshire and Somerset.

Weeks (in Ryde). Perhaps a manorial name indicating lands here once held by the Island family called *Weeks* (who may have originated from Week near St Lawrence).

Wellow (near Thorley). *Welig* c.880 (in an 11th-century copy of a Saxon charter), *Welige* 1086 (Domesday Book), *Waleia* 1189-1204, *Welewe* 1242, *Welowe* 1439. '(The place at) the willow-tree', from Old English *welig*. There are still willows here more than eleven centuries after the name was given!

Werrar Farm (1 mile south-east of Northwood). *Werore* 1199, *Werrore* c.1200, *Warrore* 1207, *Werrour* 1364, *Werrow* 1769. 'The river-bank by a weir', from Old English *wer* and *ōra*. The name must refer to a former weir in the River Medina, near to which the farm lies.

Westcliff (in Niton). *Westcliffe* 1608. Self-explanatory. In the 1608 document there is also mention of an *Estclife* 'eastern cliff'. The house called Westcliff was built in 1803.

West Court (in Shorwell). First recorded as *West Court* in the 16th century, and called *South Court* in 1608, but earlier known as *Suthshorewelle* 1316, *South Shorwelle* 1583, that is 'the south manor of Shorwell'; see North Court in the same parish. Both manors are recorded as *Sorewelle* in the Domesday Book of 1086. The word *court* is used here in the sense 'manor house'; the building itself is 16th/17th century in date.

Western Haven (near Newtown). A creek of Newtown River, partly corresponding with *Newtowne haven* 1583, *Newton haven* 1611, from Old English *hæfen* 'a harbour, a landing-place'.

West Hill (near Yarmouth). A self-explanatory name of recent origin; the hill lies west of Norton and Yarmouth.

THE DICTIONARY

Weston Manor (near Totland). *Westone* 1248, *Weston* 1280. 'The western farmstead or estate', from Old English *west* and *tūn*, so called in relation to Easton, Middleton and Norton (all in Freshwater). In medieval times the manor was known as *Weston Braybeof* 1367, *Weston Braibef* 1487, *Weston Brabeife* 1608, the manorial affix referring to the *Brayboef* family who held Weston in the 14th century.

Westover, Westover Down & Farm (near Calbourne). *Westovere* 1331, *Westouere* 1430, *Westover* 1611. 'The western ridge or bank', from Old English *west* and **ofer* or *ōfer*. The same name occurs in Somerset.

Westridge Down (near Shorwell). *Westrigge* 1293, *Westrugge* 1309, *Westrigg* 1341, *Westrygge* 1398. 'The western ridge', from Old English *west* and *hrycg*, with the later addition of *down*.

Westridge House (near Seaview). *Westridge* 1771. Probably to be identified with *Westhey* 1271, *le Westhegge* 1491, 'the western enclosure or hedge' from Old English *west* and *hæg* or *hecg*.

Westside Farm (near Chale). Named as *West Side* on Andrews's map of 1769. Self-explanatory, from its position west of Chale.

Westwood (near Wootton). A modern self-explanatory name, from its situation west of Wootton.

Whale Chine (near Chale). Recorded as *Whales Chine* in 1838, and often assumed to be so called from the stranding of a whale along the coast here at some time, like the 75-foot Greenland whale, at the nearby Blackgang Chine museum, which was wrecked on the Island in 1842. However Mr C. D. Webster points out that the chine probably takes its name from the local *Wavell* family (pronounced *Wa-ull*) who owned nearby Atherfield Farm between 1557 and 1636.

Wheeler's Bay (off Ventnor). Said to be named after Charles *Wheeler* of Ventnor, born 1824, son of John *Wheeler*, a famous smuggler at Chale. A piece of land at Ventnor was leased to a William *Wheeler* in a deed of 1840.

THE PLACE-NAMES OF THE ISLE OF WIGHT

Whippance Farm (west of Northwood). Marked as *Whippence* on Andrews's map of 1769, and to be associated with *Whippins coppes* 1608. Probably named from a family called *Whippen* or the like.

Whippingham (medieval parish, near East Cowes). *Wippingeham* 735 (in a 13th-century copy), *Wipingeham* (2), *Witingeham* (sic) 1086 (Domesday Book), *Wippingeham* 1155-8, *Wippingaham* 1193-1217, *Wyppingeham* 1227, *Whippingham* 1311. 'The homestead of the family or followers of a man called *Wippa', from an Old English personal name with *-inga-* and *hām*.

Whitcombe Manor, Great (near Carisbrooke). *Witecome* 1086 (Domesday Book), *Widecumba, Wydecumb* c.1240, *Hwytecombe* 1307, *Wydecumbe* 1329, *Whittcombe* 16th century, *Wydcomb* 1759. Probably 'the wide valley', from Old English *wīd* and *cumb*, although some spellings (including that in Domesday Book) suggest the first element may rather be Old English *hwīt* 'white'. This name may therefore be identical with Wydcombe (near Whitwell) in spite of the contrasting modern spellings.

Whitecliff Bay (in Bembridge). *la Blaunche Faloyse* 1322, *White Clyffe point* 1591, *The White Clyffe* 1611, *Whitecliff Bay* 1769. Self-explanatory, the bay taking its name from the great 'white cliff' (from Old English *hwīt* and *clif*) now known as Culver Cliff. It is called *Whitecliff or Culver Cliff* on Andrews's map of 1769. In the 14th-century document, the name appears in French.

Whitecroft Hospital (near Gatcombe). Named from *Whytecrofte* 1417, *Whitecroft* 1462, *Whitecraft* 1769, 'the white enclosure' (referring to chalky soil), from Old English *hwīt* and *croft*.

Whitefield Farm & Wood (1½ miles north of Brading). *Witesfel* (sic) 1086 (Domesday Book), *Whitefeld* 1158-61, *Witefeld* 1181, *Whytefeld* 1285, *Great & Little Whitefield* 1769. 'The white open land' (referring to chalky soil), from Old English *hwīt* and *feld*. The same name occurs in several other counties.

Whitehouse Farm (near Brading). So called in 1773, earlier *Whit house* 1664; self-explanatory.

THE DICTIONARY

Whitehouse Farm (near Porchfield). Marked as *White House* on Andrews's map of 1769. Identical in origin with the previous name.

Whiteley Bank (1½ miles east of Godshill). *Whiteley Bank* 1759, *Whetely Bank* 1769. 'The bank at the white clearing or pasture', from Old English *hwīt* and *lēah* with Middle English *banke*.

Whitwell (medieval parish, 1 mile north-east of Niton). *Quitewell* 1212, *Whytewelle* 1255, *Whitewell* 1287-90, *Whitwelle* 1357. 'The white spring or stream', from Old English *hwīt* and *wella*. The place is near the source of a small tributary of the River Yar.

Widdick Chine (in Totland). Named from *Widdick* 1837 and to be associated with *Withicke* and *Withicks glottes* (sic for *lottes* 'lots or portions of ground'). Probably from a family called *Withick* or the like who once had land here (for the surname, compare Mary *Wethick* or *Witherick* mentioned in the 1673-4 Hearth Tax returns for Newport). At an earlier date the chine seems to have been called *Whytfylde chyne* 1550 or *Whytewill Chine* 1559, perhaps named from a 'white spring' like the previous name Whitwell.

Wight, Isle of. The name of the Island itself is extremely ancient. It is recorded at a very early date, as *Vectis* in Ptolemy's Geography of c.150 AD, then as *Vecta* in the 4th-century Antonine Itinerary, as *Wiht* in Bede and the Anglo-Saxon Chronicle (9th and 10th centuries), and as *Wit* or *With* in Domesday Book (1086). In 12th- and 13th-century records it appears variously as *Wiht, With, Wicht, Wict, Wight, Wycht, Whyht, Whyt, Wyht, Wythe,* and *Wyght*. This ancient name is certainly Celtic, possibly from an old British word connected with Welsh *gwaith* 'turn, course', and its meaning may be 'place of the division', with reference to the situation of the Island between the two arms of the Solent.

Wilderness, The (1 mile south of Rookley). A stretch of land along the upper course of the River Medina, the word *wilderness* usually indicating 'barren or uncultivated land' or 'a desolate spot'.

Wilmingham (near Freshwater). *Wilmingeham* 1086 (Domesday Book), *Wilmingham* c.1225, *Wylmyngham* 1280, *Willmyngham* 1544,

THE PLACE-NAMES OF THE ISLE OF WIGHT

Wilmigem 1635. 'The homestead of the family or followers of a man called Wīghelm or Wilhelm', from an Old English personal name with *-inga-* and *hām*. The 17th-century spelling represents the local pronunciation of the name still current.

Winford (near Newchurch). *Winford* c.1246, *Wynford* c.1290, *attewenforde* 1303, *Wenford* 1608, *Winford* 1769. Probably 'the ford by the pasture or meadow', from Old English **winn* and *ford*. The 14th-century spelling occurs as a surname with Middle English *atte* 'at the'. The original ford must have been on one of the small tributaries of the River Yar just east and north of Winford.

Winkle Street (in Calbourne). Not on early record, but no doubt from Old English **wincel* 'a nook, a corner'.

Winstone Farm (near Wroxall). *Winsiston* 12th century, *Wyneston* 1287-90, *Wynestone* 1316, *Winston* 1627. 'The farmstead or estate belonging to a man called Wynsige', from an Old English personal name and *tūn*.

Wolverton Manor (near Shorwell). *Vlwarcumbe* 1086 (Domesday Book), *Wulewarton* 1189-1204, *Wlwardestone* 1235, *Woluertone* 1279, *Woolverton* 1769. 'The farmstead or estate belonging to a man called Wulfweard', from Old English *tūn* and an Old English personal name, although at the time of Domesday Book the manor seems to have been called *Vlwarcumbe*, 'Wulfweard's valley', from Old English *cumb*, referring to the valley in which Wolverton is situated. The present manor house is 16th century in date but there is evidence for earlier moated dwellings here.

Woodhouse Farm (near Whippingham). *Wodehous* 1329, *Wodehouse* 1330, *Woodhous* 15th century, *Wood House* 1769. 'The house in or near the wood', from Old English *wudu* and *hūs*.

Woodhouse Farm (south of Wootton Bridge). Recorded as *Wood House* on Andrews's map of 1769, identical with previous name.

Woodlands Vale (near Ryde). Called *Woodland's* in 1771, self-explanatory.

THE DICTIONARY

Woodside (near Wootton). Self-explanatory, one of many woodland names in this area.

Woody Bay (off St Lawrence). Self-explanatory.

Wootton (medieval parish, 3 miles west of Ryde). *Odetone* 1086 (Domesday Book), *Wudeton* 1189-1204, *Woditone* 1248, 1291, *Wotton* 1378, *Wotton bridge* 1608. 'The wooded farmstead or estate', from Old English *wudig* (adjective) and *tūn*, with the later addition of *bridge* referring to the crossing of Wootton Creek. The same name occurs in several other English counties. The area around Wootton and Wootton Bridge is still very wooded, especially to the south.

Wootton Common (near Wootton Bridge). So called on Andrews's map of 1769, alongside *Middle Common*.

Wootton Creek (near Wootton). Earlier called *Wotton hauen* 1550, *Wutton haven* 1559, *Wootton Haven* 1611, that is 'the harbour or haven of Wootton', from Old English *hæfen*. The Creek itself may have given its name to Fishbourne (on the opposite bank to Wootton), and it is in fact called *Fishborn Creek* on Andrews's map of 1775. At an earlier date, in medieval times, Wootton Creek was known as *Schaldflete* 1141-2, *Saldfluet* c.1150, *Scaudefluet* c.1260, that is 'the shallow creek', this being a duplicate of the name Shalfleet near Newtown.

Worsley Trail (a long distance trail from Brighstone to Shanklin). Named from the *Worsley* family, one of the greatest of the old Island families who for 300 years had their seats at Appuldurcombe House, now sadly a ruin, and Gatcombe House.

Wroxall (2 miles south-east of Godshill). *Wroccesheale* 1038-44, *Warochesselle* 1086 (Domesday Book), *Wroxala* 1155-60, *Wrokeshale* 1188-9, *Wroxhale* 1305, *Wroxall* 1769. 'The nook of land or secluded hollow frequented by the buzzard or other bird of prey', from Old English **wrocc* (genitive case **wrocces*) and *h(e)alh*. The same name, spelt Wraxall, occurs in Dorset, Somerset and Wiltshire.

THE PLACE-NAMES OF THE ISLE OF WIGHT

Wroxall Manor Farm (near Wroxall). Below Wroxall Down which appears as *Wroxsal Downe* 1577, *Wroxall Downe* 1617, from Old English *dūn* 'hill, down'.

Wydcombe (near Whitwell). *Wydecumbe* 1255, *Widecumbe* 1285, *Wydecoumb* 1287-90, *Wydcombe* 1565, *Whitcomb* 1769. 'The wide valley', from Old English *wīd* and *cumb*.

Yafford, Yafford House (near Shorwell). *Heceford* 1086 (Domesday Book), *Hachford* 1255, *Ecford* 1299, *Yagheford* 1408, *Yafford* 1637. 'The ford provided with a hatch or grating', from Old English *hæcc, hecc* and *ford*. The hatch would probably have been used to hold up obstructions brought down by the stream here, or to prevent animals straying up or down stream.

Yafford Mill (near Shorwell). Recorded as 'the mill of *Ocford*' (a poor spelling for *Ecford* = Yafford) as early as 1227; see the previous name.

Yar, River (flowing from Freshwater out to sea at Yarmouth). It is strange that there should be two rivers called Yar, at opposite ends of the Island. Both are so-called 'back-formations', but with quite different origins. For this 'western' River Yar; see Yarmouth.

Yar, River (flowing through Yarbridge into Bembridge Harbour). This 'eastern' River Yar is also a 'back-formation', in this case from a lost place-name *Yarneforde* near St Helens, see Yarbridge.

Yarborough Obelisk (near Culver Cliff). A memorial on Bembridge Down to Lord *Yarborough*, first Commodore of the famous Royal Yacht Squadron.

Yarbridge (in Brading). *Yarnbrigge* 1462, *Yarsbridge* 1769, *Yarbridge* 1781. 'The bridge on the River Yar', from Old English *brycg*. The river-name itself seems to be a 'back-formation' from a lost ford called *Yarneforde* 1324, 'the ford of the eagles' from Old English *earn* and *ford*, or 'the gravelly or muddy ford' if the first element is rather *$\bar{e}$aren* as in Yarmouth. The ford must have been at the mouth of the river near St Helens.

THE DICTIONARY

Yard, Upper & Lower Yard (near Godshill). *La Yerde* 1284, *atte Yerd* 1327, *Yarde* 1557, *Yard Fm* 1769. From Old English *gierd* 'a measure of land consisting of about thirty acres'. The 14th-century form occurs as a surname in which *atte* means '(living) at the'.

Yard Farm (near Wroxall). *La Ghierde* c.1227, *Yerde* 1272-9, *La Yerde* 1284, *Yerd place or Yerd ferme* 1510, *Yard* 1769. Identical in origin with the previous name.

Yarmouth (medieval parish, north of Freshwater). *Ermud* 1086 (Domesday Book), *Hernemue* c.1180, *Ernemuth* 1223, *Aremuthe* 1299, *Yaremuth* 1302. 'The gravelly or muddy river-mouth or estuary', from Old English *$\bar{e}aren$* and *$mu\bar{t}h$*. The river-name Yar is a 'back-formation' from the name Yarmouth, which came to be understood as 'the mouth of the Yar' when the original first element *$\bar{e}aren$* ceased to be meaningful. The castle here, like those at Cowes and Sandown, was built about 1546-7, in the reign of Henry VIII, to defend the coast against the French and Spanish. Yarmouth is an ancient borough, having received its charter c.1170 from Baldwin de Redvers, third Earl of Devon.

Yaverland (medieval parish, 1 mile north-east of Sandown). *Ewerelande* 683 (in a 14th-century copy), *Evreland, Everelant* 1086 (Domesday Book), *Iwerland* 1189-1204, *Euerlonde* 1291, *Yaverlond* 1324. 'The cultivated land or estate where boars are kept', from Old English *eofor* and *land*.

GLOSSARY OF THE ELEMENTS FOUND IN WIGHT PLACE-NAMES

In this list, OE stands for Old English, ME for Middle English, ModE for Modern English, and OFr for Old French. The Old English letter æ ('ash') represents a sound between *a* and *e*. The Old English letters 'thorn' and 'eth' have been rendered *th* throughout. Elements with an asterisk are postulated or hypothetical forms, that is they are words not recorded in independent use or only found in use at a later date. Place-names no longer in current use are printed in italics.

abbesse, abbodesse (ME) 'abbess'. Apesdown.

ād (OE) 'beacon'. Nodes Farm, Node's Point, The Nodes, Nodewell.

æmette (OE) 'ant'. Emmethill.

æppel (OE) 'apple'. Appley.

æsc (OE) 'ash-tree'. ?Ashey, Ashhill, Ashlake.

æscen (OE) 'growing with ash-trees'. Ashengrove.

æspe, æpse (OE) 'aspen-tree or white poplar'. Apse.

alum (ModE) 'alum'. Alum Bay.

apuldor (OE) 'apple-tree'. Appleford, Appuldurcombe.

*bagga (OE) 'bag', used either as a hill term or for the badger. ?Bagwich.

banke (ME) 'bank, hill-slope'. Whiteley Bank.

bēan (OE) 'bean'. ?Binnel, Binstead.

beau (OFr) 'fine, beautiful'. Beaper.

bench (ModE) 'flat-topped cliff'. Main Bench.

beorg (OE) 'hill, mound, barrow'. ?Bedbury, Bigbury, Gallibury, Harboro, Rowborough (2), ?Samber Hill, Summersbury.

here (OE) 'barley'. *Berdun* (the earlier name of Arreton Down), Berryl, Bierley.

*bica (OE) 'pointed ridge'. Bigbury.

THE PLACE-NAMES OF THE ISLE OF WIGHT

bierce (OE) 'birch-tree'. Birchmore.

*bil(l)ing (OE) 'ridge, hill'. Billingham.

binnan (OE) 'inside, within'. Bembridge, ?Binnel.

blæc (OE) 'black, dark-coloured'. Blackbridge, Blackgang, Blacklands, Black Pan, Black Rock Ledge, Blackwater.

blǣc (OE) 'bare of vegetation'. Bleak Down.

bord (OE) 'board, plank' or 'border'. Borthwood.

bōthl (OE) 'dwelling-place, special house or building'. Buddle.

brerd (OE) 'hill-side'. Brading.

brigdels, brīdels (OE) 'bridle'. Briddlesford.

brōc (OE) 'brook'. Brook, Carisbrooke, *Claybrook* (see Binfield), Rodge Brook, Smallbrook, Thorley Brook.

brycg (OE) 'bridge'. Bembridge, Blackbridge, Bridge, Budbridge, Coppin's Bridge, Kitbridge, Langbridge, Newbridge, Wootton Bridge, Yarbridge.

bufan (OE) 'above'. ?Bowcombe.

*bula (OE) 'bull'. Bouldnor.

burh (dative **byrig**) (OE) 'fortified place, stronghold'. Buckbury, Dunsbury, Stenbury, *Wihtwaraburh* (? an earlier name for Carisbrooke).

burh-tūn (OE) 'fortified farmstead', or 'farmstead near a fortification'. Barton Manor.

burna (OE) 'stream'. Bathingbourne, Calbourne, Debourne, Fishbourne, Osborne.

*butt (OE) 'tree-trunk, log'. ?Budbridge.

castel (ME) 'castle'. Castlehold, Cook's Castle.

cawel (OE) 'cole, cabbage'. ?Calbourne.

ceafor (OE) 'chafer, beetle'. Cheverton Down.

ceole (OE) 'throat, gorge, ravine, valley'. Chale, ?Chillerton, ?Chillingwood, ?Chilton.

*ceolle (OE) 'stream'. ?Chillingwood.

cest (OE) 'chest, coffin'. Chessell.

cinu (OE) 'chine, fissure, ravine'. Blackgang Chine, Brambles Chine, Brook Chine, Chilton Chine, Compton Chine, Grange Chine,

GLOSSARY OF THE ELEMENTS

Linstone Chine, Luccombe Chine, Shanklin Chine, Whale Chine, Widdick Chine.

cirice (OE) 'church'. Bonchurch, Churchills Farm, Newchurch.

clǣg (OE) 'clay'. *Claybrook* (see Binfield).

*****clater** (OE) 'loose stones or pebbles'. Clatterford.

clif (OE) 'cliff'. Cliff End, Cliff Farm, Culver Cliff, The Undercliff, Westcliff, Whitecliff Bay.

cniht (OE) 'young thane, retainer'. Knighton.

*****cnocc** (OE) 'hillock, knoll'. Knock Cliff.

cnoll (OE) 'hillock'. Knowles Farm.

coccel (OE) 'cockle, corncockle'. Cockleton.

cōl (OE) 'cool'. Colwell Bay.

*****corf** (OE) 'cutting, gap, pass'. Corfheath Firs, Corve.

court (ME) 'large house, manor'. Bridgecourt, Downcourt, North Court, Waytes Court, West Court.

cowe (ME) 'cow'. Cowes.

cran (OE) 'crane', also probably 'heron' or similar bird. Cranmore.

croft (OE) 'enclosure'. Whitecroft.

crokkere (ME) 'potter, maker of pots or crocks'. Crocker Street.

cros (ME) 'cross'. Lower St Cross Farm.

*****crȳde** (OE) 'weeds or other vegetation'. Cridmore.

culfre (OE) 'dove, pigeon'. Culver Cliff.

cumb (OE) 'coomb, valley'. Appuldurcombe, Bowcombe, Combley, Compton, Coombe, Gatcombe, Idlecombe, Luccombe, Nettlecombe, Rancombe, Shalcombe, Whitcombe, Wydcombe.

cweorn, cwyrn (OE) 'quern, mill'. Kern.

cyning (OE) 'king'. King's Quay, Kingston (2).

cyte, cete (OE) 'cottage'. ?Kite Hill.

cȳta, cēta (OE) 'kite'. Kitbridge, ?Kite Hill.

denu (OE) 'valley'. Dean.

dēop (OE) 'deep'. Debourne.

dierne (OE) 'hidden, secret'. *Durneford* (see Coppin's Bridge).

dover (dialect) from **douvre** (OFr) 'ridge of sand or stones', or 'salt-marsh channel'. The Duver.

THE PLACE-NAMES OF THE ISLE OF WIGHT

dūn (OE) 'hill, down'. Apesdown, Arreton Down (earlier *Berdun*), Bembridge Down (earlier *Puttokesdone*), Bleak Down, Bowcombe Down, Cheverton Down, Chillerton Down, Compton Down, Culver Down, Downcourt, Downend, Dunnose, Garstons Down, Golden Hill Fort, Head Down, Headon, High Down, Holden, Longdown, Mersley Down, Mottistone Down, Ramsdown, Rew Down, St Boniface Down, St George's Down, St Martin's Down, Sibdown, Standen, Tennyson Down, Warden Point, Week Down.

*ēaren (OE) 'gravelly, muddy'. ?Yarbridge, Yarmouth.

earn (OE) 'eagle'. ?Yarbridge.

ēast (OE) 'east, eastern'. Easton.

*ēcels, *īecels (OE) 'addition, land added to an estate'. Itchall.

elm (OE) 'elm-tree'. Elm, Elmsworth.

eofor (OE) 'boar'. Yaverland.

eowestre (OE) 'sheepfold'. Osborne.

fæger (OE) 'pleasant'. Fairlee.

feld (OE) 'open country, tract of land cleared of trees', later 'field'. Atherfield, Heathfield, Marvel, Packsfield, Porchfield, Vittlefield(s), Whitefield.

fersc (OE) 'fresh'. Freshwater.

firestone (ModE) geological term. Firestone Copse.

fisc (OE) 'fish'. Fishbourne.

*fitheling (OE) 'playing the fiddle', or 'place where a plant called **fithele* grows'. Vittlefield(s).

flēot (OE) 'inlet, creek'. Fleetlands, *Shoflet* (see King's Quay), Shalfleet, Sticelett.

flōde (OE) 'spring'. Princelett.

ford (OE) 'ford'. Appleford, Briddlesford, Clatterford, *Durneford* (see Coppin's Bridge), Farringford, Ford, Fulford, Horringford, *Huffingford* (earlier name for Blackwater), Pidford, Presford, Sandford, Scotchells Brook, Southford, Winford, Yafford.

forelande (ME) 'cape, headland, coastal promontory'. Foreland.

franche (OFr) 'free'. *Francheville* (see Newtown).

Frensche (ME) 'Frenchman'. French Mill.

GLOSSARY OF THE ELEMENTS

frogga (OE) 'frog'. Froglands.
fūl (OE) 'foul, dirty, muddy'. Fulford, Fullholding.
gafol (OE) 'tax, rent'. Golden Hill Fort.
galga (OE) 'gallows'. Gallibury, Gallows Hill.
gang (OE) 'path, track'. Blackgang.
gāra (OE) 'point of land, promontory'. Gore Cliff & Down.
gāt (OE) 'goat'. Gatcombe.
geard (OE) 'yard, enclosure'. ?Chillerton.
geat (OE), **gate** (ME) 'gate, gap, pass'. Freshwater Gate, Gatehouse.
gierd (OE) 'measure of land consisting of about 30 acres'. Yard (2).
god (OE) 'god, God'. Godshill.
grāf (OE) 'grove, copse'. Rains Grove.
grange (ME) 'outlying farm (belonging to a religious house) where crops are stored'. Combley Grange, Compton Grange, Grange.
*gyre (OE) 'marsh, mud'. Gurnard.
hæcc, hecc (OE) 'hatch, grating'. Yafford.
hæfen (OE) 'harbour, landing place'. Western Haven, Wootton Creek (earlier *Haven*).
hæg, gehæg (OE) 'enclosure'. ?Ashey, Haylands, ?Thorness.
*hær (OE) 'rock, heap of stones, cairn, tumulus'. *Etharin* (see St Helens).
hæsel (OE) 'hazel'. Heasley.
hǣth (OE) 'heath, heather'. Head Down, Headon, Heathfield.
hætt (OE) 'hat, hill'. High Hat.
hafoc (OE) 'hawk'. ?Hoxall.
hālig (OE) 'holy'. Holyrood Street.
hām (OE) 'homestead, village, manor, estate'. ?Billingham, ?Newnham, ?Sainham, Whippingham, Wilmingham.
hamm (OE) 'enclosure, land in a river-bend, river-meadow, promontory'. ?Billingham, ?Newnham, *Orham* (earlier name for Bembridge), ?Sainham, Sandown.
hām-stede (OE) 'homestead, site of a dwelling'. Hamstead.
*hānen (OE) 'stony, rocky'. Hanover Point.
hara (OE) 'hare'. Haslett.

119

THE PLACE-NAMES OF THE ISLE OF WIGHT

hēafod (OE) 'head, chief, most important'. Harboro.

hēah (OE) 'high, chief'. High Hat, High Street, High Wood.

h(e)alh (OE) 'nook or corner of land, secluded hollow'. Hale, Wroxall.

hecg (OE) 'hedge'. ?Westridge.

hēg (OE) 'hay'. Holden.

hege (OE) 'hedge'. ?Ashey, ?Thorness.

helde, hielde (OE) 'slope'. Hillway.

hīd (OE) 'hide of land'. Upper Hyde.

hlinc (OE) 'ridge, bank'. Lynch, Shanklin.

hlynn (OE) 'noisy brook or torrent'. Lynn.

hnutu (OE) 'nut'. Nettlestone.

hōh (OE) 'projecting piece of land, promontory'. Horestone Point.

hol (OE) 'hollow'. *Holloway* (earlier name for Ventnor), *Medehole* (see Osborne).

holde (ME) 'possession, tenure'. Castlehold.

holding (ME) 'holding, tenement'. Fullholding.

horn (OE) 'horn-shaped piece of land'. Horringford.

horte (OE) 'whortleberry, bilberry'. Hardingshute.

hramsa (OE) 'wild garlic'. ?Ramsdown.

hrēod (OE) 'reed, reed bed'. Landguard, Redway, Roud.

hrīs (OE) 'area of brushwood'. ?Rains Grove.

hrōc (OE) 'rook'. Rookley.

hrycg (OE) 'ridge, bank'. Ridge Copse, Rowridge, Westridge Down.

hūfe (OE) 'hood-shaped hill'. *Huffingford* (earlier name for Blackwater).

hunig (OE) 'honey'. Hunning Hall, Hunny Hill.

hūs (OE) 'house'. Woodhouse (2).

hwǣte (OE) 'wheat'. Watchingwell.

hwīt (OE) 'white'. ?Whitcombe, Whitecliff Bay, Whitecroft, Whitefield, Whitehouse (2), Whiteley, Whitwell.

hyll (OE) 'hill'. Amos Hill, Berryl, Binnel, Chessell, Churchills Farm, Doreshill, Godshill, Hill Farm (3), Hunning Hall, Hunny

GLOSSARY OF THE ELEMENTS

Hill, Kite Hill, Redhill, Lower Rill, St Catherine's Hill, Sandhills, Stoneshell.

hyrst (OE) 'wooded hill'. Parkhurst, Staplers.

-ing (OE) suffix denoting 'place belonging to, place characterized by'. ?Chillingwood, ?Dungewood, ?Hardingshute, Watchingwell.

-ing- (OE) connective particle implying 'associated with' or 'called after'. Arreton, Durton.

-inga- (OE) genitive (possessive) case of **-ingas**. Atherfield, Bathingbourne, *Huffingford* (earlier name for Blackwater), ?Chillingwood, ?Dungewood, Farringford, Horringford, Whippingham, Wilmingham.

-ingas (OE) plural suffix denoting 'people of, dwellers at'. Brading.

key (ME) 'quay'. King's Quay, Quay Street.

lacu (OE) 'stream'. Ashlake, Clamerkin Lake, Lake.

lǣce (OE) 'leech'. Leechmore.

lǣs (OE) 'pasture, meadowland'. Gotten Leaze, Lambsleaze, ?Nettlestone, ?Nunneys Wood.

lamb (OE) 'lamb'. Lambsleaze.

land (OE) 'tract of land, estate, cultivated land'. Blacklands, Fleetlands, Froglands, Haylands, Lessland, Longlands, Scotland Corner, Totland, Wackland, Yaverland.

lang (OE) 'long'. Landguard, Langbridge, Longdown, Longlands.

lēah (OE) 'wood, woodland clearing or glade', later 'pasture, meadow'. Appley, Barnsley, Bierley, Combley, Fairlee, Heasley, Holden, Kennerley, Lea, Lee, Lukely Brook, Mersley, ?Nettlestone, Rookley, Thorley, Whiteley.

litten (dialect) 'burial ground'. Church Litten.

*luca, *lūce (OE) 'river-barrier or dam'. Lukely Brook.

lufu (OE) 'love'. ?Luccombe.

*lycce (OE) 'enclosure'. Lessland.

mǣd (OE) 'meadow'. *Medehole* (see Osborne), Monktonmead Brook.

mall (ModE) 'sheltered walk serving as a promenade'. The Mall (2).

medume, meodume (OE) 'middle'. Medham, River Medina.

mere (OE) 'pool, pond'. Leechmore.

THE PLACE-NAMES OF THE ISLE OF WIGHT

merry (ModE dialect) 'black or wild cherry'. Merrie Gardens.

mersc (OE) 'marshy ground'. Marshgreen, Marsh House, Merston(e).

middel (OE) 'middle'. Middleton.

mōr (OE) 'moor, marshy ground'. Birchmore, Cranmore, Cridmore, *Lamore* (see Fulford), Moor Farm, Moortown, Padmore, Smallmoor.

mōtere (OE) 'speaker, orator'. Mottistone.

munuc (OE) 'monk'. Monks Bay, Monktonmead Brook.

mūth (OE) 'river mouth, estuary'. Hanover Point, Yarmouth.

myln (OE) 'mill'. French Mill, Mill Farm.

myrge (OE) 'pleasant, merry'. Marvel.

nǣdl (OE) 'needle'. The Needles.

netele (OE) 'nettle'. Nettlecombe.

*nīge (OE) 'new'. Niton.

*niming (OE) 'land enclosed or taken into cultivation'. Ningwood.

nīwe (OE) 'new'. Newbridge, Newchurch, Newnham, Newpark Farm, Newport, Newtown, Niton.

north (OE) 'north'. North Court, Northwood, Norton.

nose (OE) 'promontory, headland'. Dunnose.

nunne (OE) 'nun'. ?Nunneys Wood, ?Nunwell.

*ofer (OE) 'ridge, hill' or **ōfer** (OE) 'bank, shore'. Westover.

oke (ME), **āc** (OE) 'oak-tree'. Noke, ?Rock.

ōra (OE) 'shore, hill-slope'. *Orham* (earlier name for Bembridge), Bouldnor, Elmsworth, Gurnard, Werrar.

ord (OE) 'point, spit of land'. Dodnor, *Scharpenorde* (earlier name for Sconce Point), Shamblers Copse.

*padde (OE) 'toad'. Padmore.

park (ME) 'enclosed tract of land set apart for hunting'. Godshill Park, Great Park, Newpark Farm, Old Park, Park Green Farm, Park Place Farm, Parkhurst.

penn (OE) 'pen or fold for animals'. Black Pan, (Great) Pan, Walpan.

*pide (OE) 'marshy ground'. Pidford.

pīl (OE) 'post, stake'. Pyle, Pyle Street.

GLOSSARY OF THE ELEMENTS

pirige (OE) 'pear-tree'. Perreton.
place (ME) 'residence'. *Fletplace* (see Fleetlands), Pitt Place.
*plæsc (OE) 'shallow pool'. Plaish.
pōl (OE) 'pool'. Puckpool.
ponde (ME) 'pond or pool'. Pondwell.
pook (ModE dialect) 'large heap, or small rick, of hay or corn'. *Twelve Pooks* (see Deacons).
port (OE) 'harbour', or 'market town'. Newport.
prēost (OE) 'priest'. Presford, Preston.
pūca (OE) 'goblin'. Puckaster Cove, Puckwell, ?Puck House.
pund (OE) 'pound, enclosure for animals'. Pound Green.
*puttoc (OE) 'kite'. *Puttokesdone* (earlier name for Bembridge Down).
pyll (OE) 'creek, small stream'. Pell Farm.
pytt (OE) 'pit, quarry'. Pitt Place.
quarr(i)ere (OFr) 'quarry'. Quarr.
rā (OE) 'roe-deer'. Rancombe.
ræcc (OE) 'hunting-dog'. Rodge Brook.
rǣge (OE) 'female roe-deer', or 'she-goat'. ?Rains Grove.
rǣw (OE) 'row of trees, hedgerow', or 'row of houses'. Rew Farm, Rew Street.
ramm (OE) 'ram'. ?Ramsdown.
rēad (OE) 'red'. Redhill.
repaire (OFr) 'retreat'. Beaper.
rīth (OE) 'small stream'. Ryde.
road (ModE) 'sheltered water where ships may ride at anchor'. Cowes Roads.
rōd (OE) 'cross'. Holyrood Street.
rūh (OE) 'rough'. Rew Down, Rowborough (2), Rowridge.
run (ModE) 'flow or current of water'. The Run.
ryge (OE) 'rye'. Lower Rill.
salt-ærn (OE) 'building where salt is made or sold'. Saltern Wood.
sand (OE) 'sand'. ?Samber Hill, Sandford, Sandhills, Sandown.
sandig (OE) 'sandy'. Sandhills.

THE PLACE-NAMES OF THE ISLE OF WIGHT

sceald (OE) 'shallow'. Scotchells Brook, Shalcombe, Shalfleet.

sceamol (OE) 'shelf, ledge'. Shamblers Copse.

scēap-wæsce (OE) 'place for dipping sheep'. Sheepwash (2).

scearp (OE) 'sharp'. *Scharpenorde* (earlier name for Sconce Point).

scenc (OE) 'drinking cup'. Shanklin.

scīd (OE) 'plank, beam, foot-bridge'. Shide.

*scīete (OE) 'corner, nook or angle of land'. Hardingshute, Shate Farm, Sheat Manor.

scōh (OE) 'shoe, shoe-shaped spit of land'. *Shoflet* (see King's Quay).

sconce (ModE) 'small fort'. Sconce Point.

scora (OE) 'steep slope'. Shorwell.

scot (ME) 'particular payment or tax'. Scotland Corner.

scratch (dialect) 'the devil'. ?Scratchell's Bay.

scyte (OE) 'steep hill'. Barrack Shute, The Shute.

seint (ME) 'holy'. Lower St Cross Farm.

*sipe (OE) 'marshy pool'. Sibdown.

slæd (OE) 'valley'. Haslett.

smæl (OE) 'narrow'. Smallbrook, Smallmoor.

smeoru (OE) 'butter'. St Martin's Down.

smith (OE) 'smith'. ?Smithclose.

spann (OE) 'narrow strip of land, footbridge spanning a stream'. Span.

spitu (OE) 'sand-spit'. Spithead.

staca (OE) 'stake, post'. Stagwell.

stæne (OE) 'stony place'. Steyne.

stænen (OE) 'made of stone'. Stenbury.

stān (OE) 'stone'. Mottistone, Standen, Stone Farm, Stoneshell.

stapol (OE) 'post'. Staplers.

stede (OE) 'enclosed pasture, place, site'. Binstead, see also Ashengrove.

stīepel (OE) 'steep place'. Steephill.

stigel (OE) 'steep ascent'. ?Steel Bay.

GLOSSARY OF THE ELEMENTS

strǣt (OE) 'street (of houses), paved road, hamlet'. Havenstreet, High Street, Lugley Street, Pyle Street, Rew Street, South Street, Thorley Street.

strōd (OE) 'marshy ground overgrown with brushwood'. *Stroud Green* (an earlier name of Chale Green).

sumor (OE) 'summer'. Somerton, ?Summersbury.

sūth (OE) 'south'. Southford, South Street.

sūthan (OE) 'south of'. Sutton.

tēag (OE) 'small enclosure'. Tyne Hall.

thorn (OE) 'thorn'. Thorley, Thorness.

torr (OE) 'rock, rocky hill'. Puckaster Cove.

*tōt (OE) 'look-out place'. Totland.

tūn (OE) 'farmstead, village, manor, estate'. Adgestone, Afton, Alverstone (2), Alvington, Arreton, ?Bobberstone, Branstone, Brighstone, Chillerton, Chilton, Cockleton, Compton, Durton, Easton, Eddington (see St Helens), Gotten, Hulverstone, Kingston (2), Knighton, Limerstone, Linstone, Loverston, Luton, Merston(e), Middleton, Moortown, Morton, Nettlestone, Newtown, Niton, Norton, Perreton, Preston, Somerton, Sutton, Swainston, Upton, Weston, Winstone, Wolverton, *Writleston* (see Hill Farm).

under (OE) 'under, below'. The Undercliff, *Underwathe* (see St Lawrence), Under Tyne.

upp (OE) 'higher'. Upton.

ville (OFr) 'town'. *Francheville* (see Newtown).

*wacu (OE) 'watch'. Wackland.

wæd (OE) 'ford'. *Wathe* (an earlier name for St Lawrence and The Undercliff).

wæter (OE) 'water, stream, lake'. Blackwater, Freshwater.

walu (OE) 'ridge, embankment'. ?Walpan.

watershoot (ModE) 'place where water gushes out'. Watershoot Bay.

weard (OE) 'watch, look-out'. Warden Point.

weg (OE) 'way, track, road'. Hillway, Redway, *Holloway* (earlier name for Ventnor).

welig (OE) 'willow-tree'. Wellow.

THE PLACE-NAMES OF THE ISLE OF WIGHT

wella (OE) 'spring, stream'. Colwell Bay, Hoxall, Nunwell, Puckwell (see Puckaster), Shorwell, Stagwell, Watchingwell, Whitwell.

wer (OE) 'weir'. Werrar.

west (OE) 'west'. West Court, Weston Manor, Westover, Westridge Down, Westridge House.

wīc (OE) 'dwelling, specialized farm or building, dairy farm'. Bagwich, Week Farm.

wīd (OE) 'wide'. ?Whitcombe, Wydcombe.

*wierde (OE) 'watch, look-out'. *la Wyrde* (see Coombe Tower), Weards Cottage.

wilderness (ModE) 'barren land, desolate spot'. The Wilderness.

*wincel (OE) 'corner'. Winkle Street.

*winn (OE) 'pasture, meadow'. Winford.

worth (OE) 'enclosure, enclosed farmstead'. Dungewood.

writha (OE) 'something circular or curved'. ?Reeth Bay.

*writol (OE) 'babbling (spring or stream'). *Writleston* (see Hill Farm).

*wrocc (OE) 'buzzard or other bird of prey'. Wroxall.

wudig (OE) 'wooded'. Wootton.

wudu (OE) 'wood'. Borthwood, Ningwood, Northwood, Woodhouse (2).